Junior Master Gardener® presents

Wildlife Gardener℠

A JMG® Golden Ray Series℠

Level one

JuniorMaster Gardener®
growing good kids℠

NATIONAL
WILDLIFE
FEDERATION®
www.nwf.org™

Wildlife Gardener℠ produced in collaboration with the National Wildlife Federation.

Please make note of the
new website:
www.jmgkids.us/
wildlifegardener

Published and distributed by:

JMG Kids

4066 State Highway 6 South

College Station, TX   77845

(888)JMG-KIDS

www.jmgkids.org

ISBN 0-9712612-2-9

Produced by the National Junior Master Gardener® Program, Texas Cooperative Extension, The Texas A&M University System

Issued in furtherance of Cooperative Extension Work in Agriculture and Home Economics, Acts of Congress of May 8, 1914, as amended, and June 30, 1914, in cooperation with the United States Department of Agriculture, Chester P. Fehlis, Deputy Director, Texas Cooperative Extension, The Texas A&M University System.

Program Policies and Guidelines

Service marks, copyright and logos:
The terms: Junior Master Gardeners, JMG, Golden Ray Series, Wildlife Gardener and all associated logos are service marks of the Texas Cooperative Extension, College Station, Texas. Permission to use the Junior Master Gardener, JMG, Golden Ray Series and Wildlife Gardener service marks, logos and curriculum is granted to registered JMG groups of the Junior Master Gardener Program Office only.

The JMG Golden Ray Series Wildlife Gardener is copyrighted and may not be copied or duplicated without written permission from the JMG headquarters. However, any document in the appendices of the JMG Golden Ray Series Wildlife Gardener or student handouts/worksheets may be duplicated for use with the curriculum.

Commercialism: The Junior Master Gardener program is intended to be a noncommercial youth educational program. No individual associated with a JMG group, or project may enter into a contract or relationship of a commercial nature involving the JMG program unless authorized by the JMG headquarters.

No local JMG group may enter into a contract or business relationship with a business, corporation or individual that may be construed as using the JMG programs and/or their service marks, logos, names or emblems to conduct, sell or give endorsement for commercial purposes. This policy is not intended to interfere with any JMG group conducting fund-raising activities to support its local project.

Certificates and Badges: JMG Golden Ray Series certificates and/or badges are to be used only by the groups and participants of the Junior Master Gardener program. No alterations, modifications or additions to the JMG certificates and badges may be made without written permission of the JMG headquarters of Texas Cooperative Extension.

Equal Opportunity Statement:
The Junior Master Gardener program of Texas Cooperative Extension is open to all people without regard to race, color, sex, disability, religion, age or national origin.

Financial Issues: Regarding financial matters (i.e. fund-raising, accounting, banking), JMG Junior Master Gardener groups are encouraged to follow the guidelines set forth by the sponsoring organization.

Insurance: All youth groups are encouraged to secure insurance against liability and accident. Follow the procedures of the sponsoring organization for insurance guidelines and policies.

Contents

The Junior Master Gardener Program

Welcome to the Junior Master Gardener (JMG) program! JMG is a new and innovative 4-H youth gardening program that is cultivating youths, families and communities through gardening. The JMG program is growing good kids by igniting a passion for learning, success, and service.

The Junior Master Gardener Program is an international youth gardening program developed by the Texas Cooperative Extension and administered through the national Cooperative Extension network. JMG engages children in novel, "hands-on" group and individual learning experiences that promote a love of gardening, develop an appreciation for the environment, and cultivate the mind. JMG also inspires youths to be a part of service to others through service learning and leadership development projects and rewards them with certification and recognition.

The JMG program incorporates group and individual activities. Group activities can be used with a school class, JMG club, 4-H program, home school or any other group of interested young gardeners. Individual activities allow student to pursue self-directed learning at home.

Who Can start a Junior Master Gardener Group?

Any organization with a mission of youth development and education can register a JMG group, including

- Schools (i.e., public, private or home schools)

- Community/neighborhood youth programs (i.e., Master Gardener projects, scouts or church groups)

- 4-H clubs

- Boys and Girls Clubs, camps, arboreta/botanical gardens, garden clubs

How do you register as a Junior Master Gardener group?

- A minimum of five youths must be members of the group

- The group must have one or more adult leaders/teachers

- Suitable meeting facilities (i.e., classroom, garden area) must be provided

- A registration package must be properly submitted and approved

A group can enroll in the Junior Master Gardener program by completing the JMG registration packet, which can be obtained from

- A county Extension office

- The National JMG Program office at (979) 845-8565

- The appendix of this Wildlife Gardener Curriculum

- The JMG Web site at *www.jmgkids.org*

The JMG Registration Packet includes the three forms needed to organize a JMG group

- JMG Registration Agreement Form

- JMG Member Group Enrollment Form

- Leader/Teacher Registration Form

Once you receive the JMG registration packet, complete each form carefully. Mail the completed forms to the national JMG headquarters at the following address:

National Junior Master Gardener Program
225 Horticulture/Forestry Building
Texas A&M University
2134 TAMU
College Station, Texas 77843-2134

Phone (979) 845-8565
Fax (979) 845-8906

E-mail: programinfo@jmgkids.org
Web address: *www.jmgkids.org*

The National JMG Program and/or your state JMG coordinator will send an official letter of registration to your group and a copy of your registration packet will be sent to your nearest Extension office for its records. Your group of young gardeners will then be ready to begin the JMG experience.

Upon completion of this Wildlife Gardener curriculum, youths can be awarded certification as a Wildlife Gardener. Steps to registering a group and having youths earn a certification as a Wildlife Gardener are as follows:

1. Register your class or youth group as a JMG group by completing and returning the four pages of the

registration packet (located on page 167 or online at *www.jmgkids.org*). There is no cost or obligation to registering your group. Your group will receive a free and personalized registration certificate.

2. Have the class complete the following minimum requirements:

   - Complete any 12 activities from Wildlife Gardener (found on pages 1-148)

   - Complete 1 Life Skill/Career Exploration activity (found on pages 149-163)

   - Participate in 1 Community Service project(found on page 163)

3. Complete and mail in or fax completion form (located on page 175) to the National JMG Program office (address on previous page) and/or to your state JMG coordinator.

Golden Ray Series sm curricula

Completing a Golden Ray Series is a good way to recognize youths completing a small portion of the JMG program. Youths can receive Golden Ray Series certification in any of the eight chapters of the Level 1 curriculum and/or one of the stand-alone Golden Ray Series curricula, such as Health and Nutrition from the Garden or Wildlife Gardener sm.

Requirements for Golden Ray Series Certification are as follows:

- Complete any combination of 12 activities in a single chapter (from the teacher guide, youth handbook or a combination of both) or from other Golden Ray Series curricula

- Complete one Life Skill/Career Exploration activity

- Participate in one Community Service project

Habitat Garden Heroes

Some of the most useful residents in a habitat are often some of the least appreciated. There are a host of insects, spiders, reptiles, amphibians and even some mammals that serve to keep garden habitat populations of real pests in check. If you allow wildlife such as the Ground Skink, Checkered Garter Snake, Garden Spider and Silver-haired Bat to reside in a habitat, you are also welcoming these hungry consumers of flies, mosquitos, slugs, rodents and other harmful creatures. Most fears of these wildlife come from a lack of understanding of these often unappreciated creatures.

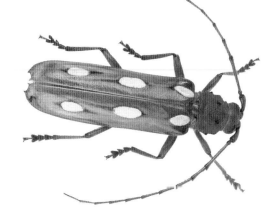

Here are some points to remember

1. All wildlife, from common garter snakes to cotton-tailed rabbits, should be viewed only from a distance. Remember that these are wildlife. Their space should be respected. It is never a good idea to try to hand feed or handle any wildlife in your garden habitat.

2. Of the 250 species of snakes in the United States, only a small fraction are venomous. If you are concerned about venomous snakes, first learn if there are any of these species of snakes in your area by visiting links available at *www.jmgkids.org/wildlifegardener*. If you see a snake in your garden habitat, remember that it is most likely a harmless species that eats rodents, frogs, insects or birds and is doing its part to keep the habitat in a natural balance.

3. Many of these creatures have likely already existed in your area peacefully for quite some time. Because many of these wildlife are fearful of human activity and are usually more active at night, there is a good chance you haven't and probably won't cross paths very often!

Introduction to Native Plants

A native plant is a species that naturally occurs on a site and has not been introduced from another region or country. Native plants thrive in their

natural setting without disrupting natural ecological processes because they are perfectly adapted to the conditions of that locale. Native plants provide the best diversity of habitat elements for wildlife. Wildlife species have evolved to rely upon native plants as food, cover and sometimes even for water. The National Wildlife Federation and Junior Master Gardener strongly encourages the use of native plant species in all new plantings.

By choosing native plants for your Schoolyard Habitats site, you

- provide less water and overall maintenance

- require less water and overall maintenance

- provide excellent support to local wildlife species

- help maintain the diversity of plant species in your community

The wildlife in our communities flourish amid locally native plants. However, there are hundreds of species of exotic plants originally from Asia, Europe, Africa, and Australia that are available for sale and now call the landscapes of North America home. These plants do not sustain local wildlife as well as native plants do. Though these plants may offer birds fruit, squirrels nuts, and hummingbirds and butterflies nectar, they do not provide the full range of seasonal habitat benefits that appropriate locally native species provide. If we want to attract wildlife and restore the critical, often unseen small pieces in our ecosystems, we need to bring back locally native plants.

An equally important reason to use locally native plants is to reduce the possibility that exotic plants from our landscapes will run wild. Native plants do not become invasive; that is, they will not reproduce rampantly, invading and impoverishing the diversity of our remaining natural habitats (as an increasing number of exotic plants now do). Non-native plants often reproduce quickly, depleting the diversity of remaining natural habitats. When a non-native species is planted in a new place, it is isolated from its original region or country and the controls present there including insects and diseases that limited its spread in its place of origin. This lack of controls in a new area often allows the plant species to spread unchecked in its new environment.

Rapidly growing and reproducing exotics often displace native plants that cannot compete with them. Consequently, animals that depend on native plants to provide a particular habitat component may not find a suitable replacement among the non-native species. Exotic plants that have been popular in formal landscaping but which have been particularly invasive in many parts of the U.S. (and therefore should not be planted) include purple loosestrife, multiflora and Cherokee roses, Asiatic bush honeysuckle, Japanese honeysuckle, nandina, privet, autumn, Russian olive and burning bush euonymus, and many others. NWF and your local native plant societies can provide region-specific plant lists to assist with your plant selections.

Locally native plant species meet virtually any landscaping need. By choosing native species, you will replace the monotony of the few exotics that dominate our landscapes and the spread of exotic invasives that are choking out the diversity of local plants in woodlands, roadsides, meadows and natural ecosystems.

Our landscapes, carefully planted with locally native species, can be effective instruments in restoring native plants to our communities and open spaces.

Most local nurseries and plant centers sell native plants, whether they know it or not. Because some nursery staff may not be familiar with native plants and their benefits, educating yourself about the plants you would like to purchase prior to visiting the nursery is helpful. Many nurseries are willing to special-order plants that they do not normally stock. If possible, request your plants by species name rather than common name, as one common name is often ascribed to many different species. Your state native or wildflower society is the best sources of finding reputable native plant suppliers in your area.

NWF and Schoolyard Habitats

National Wildlife Federation® Mission Statement

The mission of the National Wildlife Federation is to educate, inspire and assist individuals and organizations of diverse cultures to conserve wildlife and other natural resources and to protect the Earth's environment in order to achieve a peaceful, equitable and sustainable future.

The Schoolyard Habitats® Program:

The National Wildlife Federation (NWF)'s Schoolyard Habitats program assists formal and non-formal educators, youth, schools and youth service organizations and community members in the creation and restoration of wildlife habitat and in the use of the school/facility grounds as outdoor classrooms for interdisciplinary learning/programming.

Why should we make this effort to help songbirds, butterflies, and other wildlife with whom we share our communities? Habitat loss is the greatest threat to biodiversity — the grand variety of life forms that live on Earth. No matter where we are, we can take small actions in our daily lives to make a positive impact on our local environment. At our schools, community centers and learning centers, we have a chance, and perhaps an obligation, to put our youth in contact with the natural world. The Schoolyard Habitats program offers this opportunity while enhancing the quality of education in our schools, after-school programs and communities.

Who Can Create a Schoolyard Habitat?

- After-school Programs
- Nature Centers
- Parks
- Community and Recreation Centers
- Camps
- Day Care Centers
- Museums and Botanical Gardens
- Preschools
- Boys and Girls Clubs
- YMCAs and YWCAs

- Libraries

- Faith-based Organizations

- Zoos and Aquariums

- Any Youth Service Organizations

To date, NWF has certified nearly 2,000 sites across the country. In addition to schools, any group or individual interested in working with youth and teens to create wildlife habitat sites on their facility grounds may apply.

Project Size and Scope

The size and scale of Schoolyard Habitat sites vary greatly. Sites can be created on a rooftop, in a series of containers or on any available land your facility may have. The size and design of the habitat site is up to you and the participants. Whether you are in an urban, rural or suburban area, you can create a wildlife habitat site that meets the needs of your school, program and local wildlife.

The Benefits of Creating a Schoolyard Habitats Site

Schoolyard Habitat sites meet the needs of wildlife by providing the four critical habitat components: food, water, cover and places to raise young. These projects offer many benefits to students and educators, including enhanced hands-on learning opportunities, on-site "field trips," decreased grounds maintenance costs, development of stronger ties within the community and a sense of empowerment and environmental stewardship in their own neighborhoods and beyond. Schoolyard Habitat sites

offer unlimited cross-curricular learning and provide a creative tool with which educators can meet state and national standards of learning while meeting the needs of diverse learning styles.

Additional benefits of creating Schoolyard Habitats sites include:

- Enhanced programming options (environmental club, nature art class, bird watching, etc.)

- Opportunities for intergenerational programming and/or mentoring

- Neighborhood beautification

- Increased community and parental involvement

- Skill development, including team building, decision making, leadership, character development and school-to-work skills

- Community service and service learning opportunities

- Alignment of an existing curriculum with National Science Standards

- Valuable habitat for local wildlife

For the youth involved, creating and maintaining a habitat project provides a dynamic, relevant, real-world learning experience. Creating or restoring a habitat not only gives students a hands-on opportunity to learn about wildlife, but also empowers them to create positive change and take an active role in their schools, neighborhoods and communities. Working on a Schoolyard Habitats project allows students to discover how they can make a difference. Reinforcing these lessons with awareness activities and continued project upkeep develops students' sense of stewardship for the natural world.

For additional information on the Schoolyard Habitats program visit us on the web at *www.nwf.org/schoolyardhabitats*

JMG/NWF Partnership

The Junior Master Gardener® Program and the National Wildlife Federation® have partnered to bring the wonders of gardening for wildlife to America's youths. This partnership educates youth across the country about the importance of conserving and restoring wildlife habitat in their own gardens and communities. For more information about this partnership, the National

Wildlife Federation, the Junior Master Gardener Program or to learn about opportunities to take part in teacher workshops or other special events, visit *www.nwf.org/schoolyardhabitats* or *www.jmgkids.org/wildlifegardener*.

What is a Wildlife Gardener₅ₘ?

Many adults enjoy working and relaxing in the outdoors; garden settings provide youths with the same types of simple pleasures. Many children today have not had the opportunity to experience the sense of responsibility that comes from nurturing a fragile seedling or the amazement that grows from watching that seedling develop into a towering sunflower. They do not know the wonder that comes from watching a mother bird feeding her young or watching a spider methodically weaving a web.

Whether it's a pair of squirrels chasing each other through the trees or a chorus of frogs and songbirds that help rid the garden of harmful insects, wildlife can be a welcome addition to any garden setting. This curriculum is a resource to help youths understand wildlife and their needs while learning to appreciate the contribution and their aesthetic value to a garden habitat.

This JMG Golden Ray Series curriculum, Wildlife Gardener engages children in outdoor activities and exploration. It increases environmental awareness and allows children to learn responsibility in caring for living things. While teaching children to be patient in working towards a very rewarding end, your students will learn to identify and understand forms of wildlife they may encounter in a garden habitat. Your Wildlife Gardeners will be able to recognize the basic components of habitat and learn how to incorporate those components into a garden setting to attract desirable wildlife to their wildlife garden.

The JMG Wildlife Gardener curriculum contains dozens of hands-on activities designed for youths grades 3-5. This activity guide provides youths, in formal and non-formal educational settings, with hands-on opportunities to explore the natural world and activities that encourage leadership development, personal pride, responsibility, and

community involvement. Along with developing critical thinking skills, youths will identify local conservation concerns and take action to address them through individual and group projects. This curriculum allows kids to become certified Wildlife Gardeners. Students will also have the opportunity to take part in a service-learning project by creating National Wildlife Federation® certified Schoolyard Habitats® and Backyard Wildlife Habitat™ sites.

Benefits of gardening for wildlife

Your schools and community will reap many benefits from engaging in wildlife gardening, including

- Providing easy access, on-site field trips

- Empowering students

- Providing long-term involvement and access to a natural place

- Affirming a place and role for humans in the environment

- Demonstrating student ability to make a difference

- Building community

- Restoring the local environment

- Transforming and beautifying the schoolyard

- Reducing landscape maintenance needs (labor and costs)

- Providing a context for teaching across all subject areas

- Increasing safety and productive use of schoolyard

- Promoting physical and mental health and well-being (both through the physical activity associated with garden work and the peacefulness the habitat area provides)

- Providing good opportunities for creating positive social relationships across the school community

- Promoting high levels of student achievement

- Providing new ways to meet the needs of all students

What is Service-Learning?

Service-learning combines service to the community with student learning in a way that improves both the student and the community. According to the National and Community Service Trust Act of 1993, Service-Learning can be defined as follows:

- Is a method whereby students learn and develop through active participation in thoughtfully organized service that is conducted in and meets the needs of communities

- Is coordinated with an elementary school, secondary school, institution of higher education, or community service program and the community

- Helps foster civic responsibility

- Is integrated into and enhances the academic curriculum of the students, or the education components of the community service program in which the participants are enrolled

- Provides structured time for students or participants to reflect on the service experience

How can my kids become Certified Wildlife Gardeners?

Check each step below:

☐ **Register your group.**

By completing the registration on pages 167-175 your group will become a registered JMG Group.

Registering your class or youth group is FREE and the National JMG Program office with list your group online and send your group a free, personalized certificate recognizing your JMG Group! If you have any questions about registering your JMG Group, call the National Junior Master Gardener Program office at 979-845-8565 or email us at *programinfo@jmgkids.org*

☐ **Group completes at least 12 activities from the first seven teaching/learning concepts .**

These can be a total of any 12 or more activities from Activity 1 (P.L.A.N.T. and Wildlife Needs) through Activity 36 (Backyard Buddy)

☐ **Group completes at least one activity from the Life Skills and Career Exploration teaching/learning concepts. (pages 149-163)**

☐ **Group completes at least one Service Learning/Leadership Development project. (page 163)**

Your group will likely be implementing components of habitat as you complete activities of the Wildlife Gardener curriculum. Having your group establish and certify a site as a National Wildlife Federation Certified Schoolyard Habitat is the perfect culminating experience! See Schoolyard Habitats Certification on pages 219-226 for more information.

Your group may also create your own service-learning project that incorporates what your group has learned through their Wildlife Gardener experiences! Involve your Wildlife Gardeners in helping to identify what particular needs might exist in your community then decide on a project, plan how it will be accomplished and implement the plan.

☐ **Return completion form. (page 175)**

Upon completion of this Wildlife Gardener curriculum, youths in registered JMG groups will earn a Golden Ray Series certification as a Wildlife Gardener. There is no cost for certification and personalized certificates for each Certified Wildlife Gardener will be mailed directly to you.

Youths can also be awarded Wildlife Gardener Recognition Medals for completing portions of Wildlife Gardener. More information about recognition medals can be found on page 18.

Habitat Gardening Basics

As your group begins working to complete activities in its study as Wildlife Gardeners, consider having students keep a journal to write in following each activity. This could be in the form of a simple notebook or folder decorated in a Wildlife Gardener theme. Have them record what the group did, what they learned from the activity, and what their response to the activity was (in other words, how they felt about what they learned, their opinions about what they are learning about, their hopes about what the group will be doing, etc.). A journal is a great way for kids to review concepts in their own minds while giving them a chance to reflect on their experience.

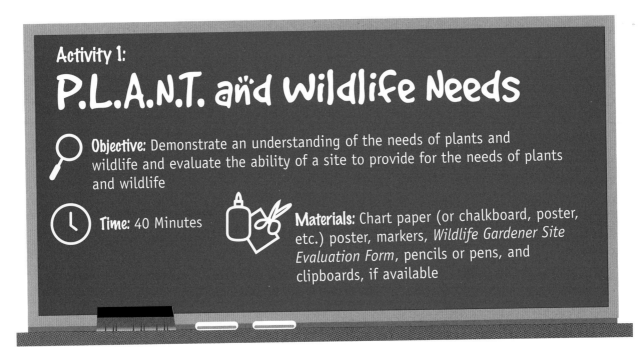

Activity 1:
P.L.A.N.T. and Wildlife Needs

Objective: Demonstrate an understanding of the needs of plants and wildlife and evaluate the ability of a site to provide for the needs of plants and wildlife

Time: 40 Minutes

Materials: Chart paper (or chalkboard, poster, etc.) poster, markers, *Wildlife Gardener Site Evaluation Form*, pencils or pens, and clipboards, if available

*NOTE: This introductory activity focuses on helping your gardeners to begin to understand the needs of plants and wildlife while thinking about the type of wildlife your group wants to welcome to the garden area. The lesson taps background knowledge and helps students begin thinking about all of the elements of gardening for wildlife and establishing a habitat. As your group thinks about the wildlife they want to attract and learns more about establishing a habitat for both plants and animals, they can add features not already at the site, including food, a source of water, shelter, and protective cover for wildlife to raise their young. **This activity is complimented by the Habitat Tag on page 20.***

Prior to this session, select three locations as possible areas to establish a garden/habitat area. Use the Wildlife Gardener Site Evaluation form as a guide. Ideally you'll select one or two of the possible sites to be desirable locations while the others may not be as suitable. (See Appendix page 177, Garden Planting and Prepping Instructions for more information)

Start a discussion of what people need to live: food, water, air, shelter and clothing. Ask a student to point out from the list those items they think plants must have to be able to live. Ask if they know of anything that plants need that people do not. On the left side of the chart paper, write the acronym "P.L.A.N.T.S" in a column and list the need that each letter represents. Complete the chart shown on the next page and challenge learners to recall the list of plant needs without looking.

1

Plant Needs

P lace – a container, garden or other place for roots to grow

L ight – sun or artificial light

A ir – oxygen and carbon dioxide

N utrients – nitrogen, phosphorous, potassium and others

T hirst – plants, like all living things, need water

S oil – soil or other media for roots to grow

Next ask the group to think about the basic needs of people and which of those needs are shared with

the group to suggest examples of how different animals have these needs met and write them beside that need. Ask the group what the need "shelter" represents. Explain to the group that as Wildlife Gardeners, they will be trying to find and create shelter for wildlife that they will look for two kinds of shelter: shelter that provides cover and shelter that provides places to raise young.

Take the group outside to begin thinking about where the garden habitat area could be established. Tell the students that as Wildlife Gardeners they are going to learn

Shelter

Cover provides wildlife a quick place to hide from predators and other dangers and also provides a hiding place to help in hunting prey.

Places to raise young are places to care for young animals

Wildlife Needs

Food – berries, juicy leaves, insects

Water – rain water, water from puddles, bird baths

Air – they breathe the same air we do!

Shelter (Cover) – under big rocks, inside old logs

(Places to raise young) – nests in trees, under water

wildlife. Create the list (food, water, air, shelter, and clothing) on chalkboard or chart paper. Have students circle the items that are also needs of animals. Ask

about different forms of wildlife and make decisions how to create a garden area that provides for plant and animal needs.

Point out that most plants do well if the garden site is sunny, the ground well drained and the garden is near a water source that is easy to get to.

The best location for wildlife includes the following elements:

A Variety of Plants, including grasses, small plants, shrubs and trees.

Sources of Food, such as insects, berries, and leaves, and a variety of other plant material.

Shelter that Provides Cover, such as big rocks, old logs and a variety of other plant material.

Shelter that Provides Places to Raise Young, including shallow pools of water, dense grasses, shrubs, trees, etc.

Remind the group they are also evaluating the area and they should rate each criterion. Pass out copies of the *Wildlife Gardener Site Evaluation* form. If possible, equip each student with clipboard and as a group, visit each of the three possible locations you selected. Lead the group in pointing out elements of food, water, and shelter. Tell the group they are scientists evaluating the area and they should rate each criterion and then check each of the basic needs for wildlife that the area already provides.

Once students have rated each criterion, they should add the scores for each site and write the total in the flower.

Plant and Wildlife Needs Discussion Questions

1. Which site is most suitable for the garden habitat?

2. Did everyone select the same site? What are some of your reasons for recommending other sites?

Listen to all students' thoughts and opinions and lead the group to consensus on the best location of the site.

Wildlife Gardener Site Evaluation Form

Name:

You are trying to decide on the best place to grow a garden for wildlife. Circle one number for each line, with 5 meaning "best" and 1 meaning "worst".

Location of Site 1: _____

Area has both sunny and shaded areas	1	2	3	4	5
Area is near water source	1	2	3	4	5
Area is easy for your group to get to	1	2	3	4	5
Variety of plants *(including grasses, small plants, shrubs and trees)*	1	2	3	4	5
Source of Food	1	2	3	4	5
Shelter that Provides Cover	1	2	3	4	5
Place to Raise Young	1	2	3	4	5

What was that site's score?

Location of Site 2: _____

Area has both sunny and shaded areas	1	2	3	4	5
Area is near water source	1	2	3	4	5
Area is easy for your group to get to	1	2	3	4	5
Variety of plants *(including grasses, small plants, shrubs and trees)*	1	2	3	4	5
Source of Food	1	2	3	4	5
Shelter that Provides Cover	1	2	3	4	5
Place to Raise Young	1	2	3	4	5

What was that site's score?

Location of Site 3: _____

Area has both sunny and shaded areas	1	2	3	4	5
Area is near water source	1	2	3	4	5
Area is easy for your group to get to	1	2	3	4	5
Variety of plants *(including grasses, small plants, shrubs and trees)*	1	2	3	4	5
Source of Food	1	2	3	4	5
Shelter that Provides Cover	1	2	3	4	5
Place to Raise Young	1	2	3	4	5

What was that site's score?

Which site had the highest score?   1   2   3

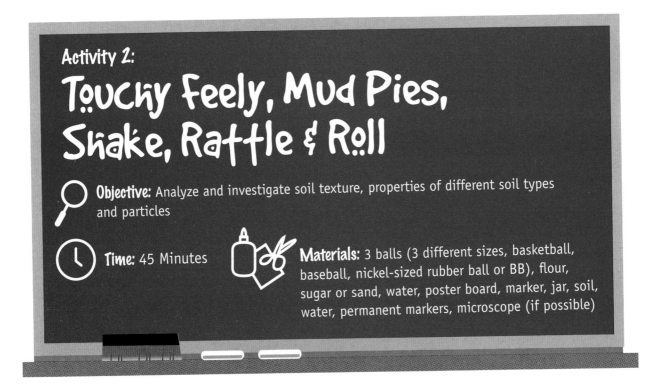

Activity 2:
Touchy Feely, Mud Pies, Shake, Rattle & Roll

Objective: Analyze and investigate soil texture, properties of different soil types and particles

Time: 45 Minutes

Materials: 3 balls (3 different sizes, basketball, baseball, nickel-sized rubber ball or BB), flour, sugar or sand, water, poster board, marker, jar, soil, water, permanent markers, microscope (if possible)

NOTE: *Just because a plant is provided the right amount of light, water and nutrients, is no guarantee it will grow to be healthy and highly productive. The soil that houses the plant is just as important, if not more so, as the other basic needs. A plant must be able to adsorb nutrients and water from the soil; otherwise, a garden will not flourish. Below are three different kid-friendly tests for investigating your soil. Have fun and consider completing these activities outdoors - they tend to be messy and fun learning experiences!*

Touchy Feely

Discuss with students some of the things they have learned about plant needs. What do they think will happen if a plant's roots are always dry or always sopping wet? To make sure that the roots of the plants stay healthy, you need to have good soil. On a sheet of poster board titled "SOIL – What's In It?," have students list what they think they would find in soil if they started digging. Answers may include dirt, clay, water, sand, trash, roots, bugs, etc. Write down all answers, even if not completely correct. The list will be modified later.

When the list is complete, discuss the ingredients in soil. One component of soil is small pieces of rock called particles. There are three main kinds of particles, and they are different sizes. The three soil particles are sand, silt and clay. One of the main differences between these particles is their size. Explain that if they could look at soil under a microscope, sand would be the biggest. A great way to convey the relative size of these particles to each other is to use balls! Show them the largest ball. The next smaller particle is silt. It is small. Show them the medium sized ball. The smallest particle is clay. It is tiny. Show them the smallest ball.

Explain that these three balls demonstrate the difference in the proportion of the particles to each other.

Explain to the group that soil that is very sandy does not usually grow plants very well. This is because it dries out quickly and does not let roots get enough water. Allow each student to feel the sugar particles which are about the same size and texture as sand, and have them describe it to you. Allow them to feel the dry flour and rub it between their fingers to understand the silky, powdery texture of silt.

Clay particles are very fine textured. They clump together and become slick and sticky. Soil that has mostly clay does not allow plants to grow well because there is very little air space between the tiny clay particles. Clay soils tend to be hard and compacted when dry, waterlogged and drain poorly when wet, making it difficult for plant roots to grow. Let students feel flour with a little water mixed in to feel the sticky texture of clay.

If possible, allow students to locate actual samples of soil particles and view them under a microscope or using a magnifying glass.

Mud Pies

Tell the students they are going to make mud pies to determine if the garden soil has good texture. Ask them to help you dig a hole in the area the group has chosen to use for their garden. The soil taken out of the hole should be enough

for everyone to make get a handful of soil. Scrapping the soil off the top does not give gardeners a true sample of their garden's soil texture. Rather, dig the hole down into the soil at least six inches from the top. Mix the sample together well to make a homogenous mixture. Add a little water to the soil and squeeze it together forming a mud pie (add just enough water for the soil to stick together. It should not ooze through your fingers but should make a good mud ball).

Have the gardeners make an educated guess of the soil's texture.

- If the pie is crumbly and falls completely apart, the soil has a sandy-texture.

- If it is sticky, glistens and keeps its shape, it's a clay soil.

- If the ball is loose, crumbly, and not sticky, the soil is a loam soil.

Shake, Rattle & Roll

Tell them it's now time to determine if their guess is right! Use some of the remaining mixture to fill a large jar half-full with the mixture and fill remaining space with water. Have the gardeners take turns vigorously shaking the jar until the larger clumps are broken apart. Let the jar sit for two minutes. Use a permanent marker to draw a line to mark what has settled. Remind gardeners that sand makes up the heaviest particles, so it sinks to the bottom the quickest. Allow at least 24 hours without moving the jar for the mixture to

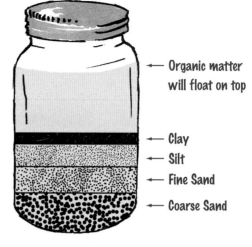

← Organic matter will float on top

← Clay
← Silt
← Fine Sand
← Coarse Sand

settle further. The top layer will be clay, which includes the smallest, lightest particles. The middle layer will be silt, and the bottom will be sand. Have the gardeners decide which layer is the thickest to determine the soil's texture.

As the group completes all 3 tests, ask them to determine if their findings were consistent. Were they able to determine the soil type? Remind the group that regardless of a soil's texture, organic matter can improve it to make it more plant friendly!

The best soil will contain an even mixture of sand, silt, and clay. This is called a **loam** soil.

In the Classroom

Have the students graph the height of the separate layers in centimeters. Then have the group break into small groups. Have them duplicate the *Shake, Rattle & Roll* activity with soil from different areas and record and graph their findings. The groups should then present their findings to the rest of the JMG group. Ask children if they think this activity might influence where they might place a garden habitat.

Activity 3:
Small and Large

Objective: Demonstrate understanding of spacing requirements when planting seeds and transplants

Time: 50 Minutes   **Materials:** None needed

If students will be adding new plant material to their wildlife garden, whether they use seeds or transplants, have them think about how the garden should be arranged. Ask what they think will happen if all were planted too closely together. Guide them in a discussion that plants have many needs (see P.L.A.N.T. and Wildlife Needs activity, page 2) and they must have enough space to ensure all these needs can be met. If plants are planted too close, they might not all get enough light or water or other requirements.

Ask four group members to volunteer to be wildflowers in a Wildlife Garden. Have them sit on the floor next to one another in a square and stretch out their arms and fingers as if they are growing toward the light. Ask 6 additional members to be tall sunflowers and stand closely around the wildflower plants so they are crowded. Have the sunflowers stretch their arms up and grow, too. The wildflowers should be feeling crowded

at this point. Ask they feel they are getting enough light. Roots from the sunflowers will probably grow all around the wildflowers, soaking up water. Ask the rest of the class to suggest ways to rearrange the sunflowers and wildflowers so that they have enough space to grow, but not so much space that weeds are given ample room to grow.

Next, add a few more members to the plant group. The newest members are medium-sized shrubs. Tell the group to imagine that these were planted when the shrubs were small, but the tags on the plants were not even looked at when they were planted. It didn't take long for them to grow into more area and become too crowded. Explain that it is important to know about how big a plant is going to be when it becomes mature. Point out that almost any plant they would want to purchase will come with information about the plant including its size it will reach at maturity.

Have the class talk about on an appropriate arrangement and spacing for the plants, ask them decide which side of the garden is the front side. Explain that gardens are arranged with consideration for visual appeal as well as spacing and shading. Taller plants are usually arranged at the back, medium height plants are placed in the middle, while shorter plants are placed in the front. Have them rearrange one final time with these considerations in mind.

Explain to the group that they will need to keep these points in mind as they begin to decide on what plants to use and where they will be placing them in future Wildlife Gardener activities and projects.

In the Classroom

Use grid paper to sketch a 5"x10" grid (or as a group create a larger grid on a chalkboard or poster board) to represent a small garden area. Have the students help you create a map of their "people" garden by adding the final arrangement of wildflowers, sunflowers and shrubs. Explain that each square on the map represents one square foot in the garden. Have the group determine the area of the grid by counting the squares or multiplying two adjoining sides. For this exercise they should use symbols to draw each plant so that

- Each sunflower is allowed 1 square foot.

- Each shrub is allowed 4 square feet.

- Two wildflowers are allowed for each square foot.

Activity 4:
Rules-n-Tools

Objective: Establish safety practices for the garden learning area

Time: 45 Minutes

Materials: Poster board or construction paper, markers

As the garden is being developed, ask students come up with a list of garden rules that will make the garden a safer place for the people in it and for the plants. Brainstorm rules with the students. Pose the following situations to guide them in developing rules for their garden.

Garden Situations

- Someone is running through the garden habitat and accidentally runs over and crushes a plant.

- A student is playing with a shovel by spinning it in the air and hits another person in the back.

- A student is walking on the timbers edging the garden, stumbles, and falls into and breaks a bird bath.

- The JMG group arrives at their garden to find that the tools were left out all night. The wheel barrow has been stolen and some of the other tools are beginning to rust.

- A boy is pulling weeds and raking the soil. He lays the rake down with the sharp tines pointed up so that he can pull another weed. A girl walks by and steps on the rake. The tines stick into her sandals and cut her foot.

- A team is watering the garden. They are talking to each other while the leader is telling them how much plant food to put in the watering can. The group isn't listening and puts too much plant food on the plants. Some of the plants die.

Try to keep the garden rules to 6-7 or less. Have the class decide on the most important rules from their lists, and have students work in partners to make a Garden Rules poster. Encourage students to make their posters colorful and to include illustrations if they'd like.

Rules-n-Tools Discussion Questions

1. What rules do you follow at home or at school? What happens if you don't follow the rules?

2. Why do we have rules?

3. Do you think our garden would work as well if we had no rules?

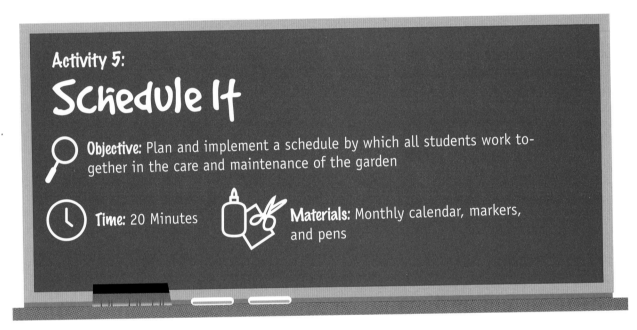

Activity 5:
Schedule It

🔍 **Objective:** Plan and implement a schedule by which all students work together in the care and maintenance of the garden

🕐 **Time:** 20 Minutes

Materials: Monthly calendar, markers, and pens

Ask the group to tell you what they do when they are thirsty. Explain that while they have the ability to get up and get a drink of water, garden plants don't. Ask the group how often they think plants in a garden need to be watered. Explain that different plants need different amounts of water but most usually do best if the soil stays moist. Tell the group that successful gardeners need a water source they can access on a regular basis.

Discuss the garden's maintenance needs with students. Do they think that their plants need to be taken care of everyday? Will their garden need to be watered and weeded everyday? What about fertilizing? Explain that even though the garden probably will not need care on a daily basis, it is a good idea to check plants regularly for signs of drying out and for weeds popping up.

Tell students that they are going to make a schedule that ensures regular care of the garden by all students. Divide students into groups, and have each group come up with a name for their

1

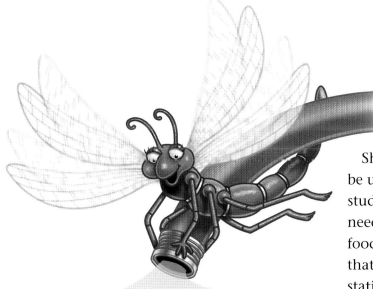

group. These will be the garden maintenance teams that take turns caring for the garden.

Show students a calendar that will be used as a master schedule. Prompt students to list tasks that are most needed—watering, giving plants plant food (fertilizing), and weeding. Tell them that the plants and wildlife watering stations (such as birdbaths other water sources) need to be checked every other day.

Hand watering or using a soaker hose works well in small gardens. With hand watering, half-gallon or gallon jugs can be filled at a sink or hose and carried back and forth to the garden. If the water has to be transported from inside or carried a long distance, use a cart or wagon to transport several jugs at a time. Show students how to slowly water at the base of the stem and water plants one-by-one. Soaker hoses are also effective means of irrigation. They are made of spongy, porous material that releases water slowly along the length of the hose. The hose can be laid alongside a row of plants, turned on, and left for a half hour or longer. This allows water to soak into the soil thoroughly to a depth of several inches, and channels the water to the plant's roots, where it is needed most. (This conserves water and avoids muddy messes!)

The best way to check for a plant's watering needs is to stick their finger into the dirt approximately one inch deep (about the length from the tip of their finger to their first knuckle). If the soil feels dry at that depth, it needs to be watered. Have a student draw in a blue water drop on every Monday, Wednesday and Friday to signify a watering day. Next, have a member of each team come up and take turns

writing their team's name by a watering day. They will be responsible for watering on these days.

If your group will be fertilizing plants in the garden habitat, mark one of the watering days each week as a fertilizer day as well. An easy way to fertilize is to use a water-soluble fertilizer. Explain that is very important to carefully follow directions. Most water-soluble fertilizers can be easily spooned into jugs as students fill them, and the plants get fertilized as they are being hand watered. (Note: If you use a granular fertilizer that is sprinkled onto the soil instead of a water-soluble fertilizer, it does not need to be applied every week. Read the label carefully and schedule fertilizer applications according to directions.)

The last task to be added to the schedule is weeding. This needs to be done once or twice a week to keep ahead of weeds. Explain that weeds steal the water, light and space that their vegetables need. Decide on a symbol for weeding and pick a day of the week to do it. Again, have groups take turns signing up for weeding times. Demonstrate how to pull a weed, and explain that they should try to pull up the weed's roots when they pull up the rest of the plant. Caution students to be careful not to pull up plant seedlings that they are trying to grow!

Praise the group for their organizational and planning efforts. Point out that their team schedules ensure that the garden area does not receive too little care or too much water and fertilizer and that weeds will be kept in check.

In the Classroom

Have the class use a calendar to answer the following questions:

- How many months are in a year? What are they?
- How many weeks are in a year?
- How many days are in a year?
- How many watering days will our group water this year?
- How many weeding days will our group weed this year?
- How many fertilizing days will our group fertilize this year?

1

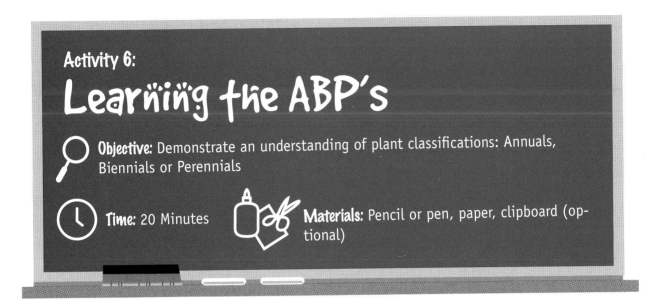

Activity 6:

Learning the ABP's

Objective: Demonstrate an understanding of plant classifications: Annuals, Biennials or Perennials

Time: 20 Minutes

Materials: Pencil or pen, paper, clipboard (optional)

Kids at this age know their ABC's, but most don't know their ABP's. Explain that ABP represents the three main kinds of plants that people can put in their gardens: annuals, biennials, and perennials. Write the three words on a poster or chalkboard. Ask the group if they have any ideas about what the words might mean.

Tell the gardeners that you are going to give them some hints — underline the word "annual" and tell the group that this word means "once a year." Tell them when you are talking about plants, an annual plant is one that grows and dies all in one year.

Underline the prefix *BI* in biennial. Tell them the word bicycle also starts off with the prefix *BI* because it has two wheels; explain that when we are talking about plants, a biennial is a plant that grows for two seasons instead of just one (like an annual). Biennials are less common than other plant types.

Ask them how long they think a perennial lives. Tell the group that perennial plants are special because they can last for many years. Explain that sometimes the top part of some perennials will die back if it gets too cold. When it does this, the bottom part of the plant continues to live and will grow a new set of stems and leaves when the weather warms back up.

If possible, take the group to a nursery or any place where a variety of plants are on display, or arrange for a visit from someone from a nursery or your county Extension office. Ask the experts to share with the group the difference between annuals, biennials and perennials. Have the group read the tags to find out common names, scientific names and plant types. List the different annuals, perennials and biennials the group finds.

As students begin selecting plants to be a part of garden habitat, explain the

value of including different types of plants, especially annuals and perennials. Perennials often add stability to a garden area by remaining green for longer periods of time (even year around). Annuals require planting each year but add great color and are usually easy to grow, even from seeds.

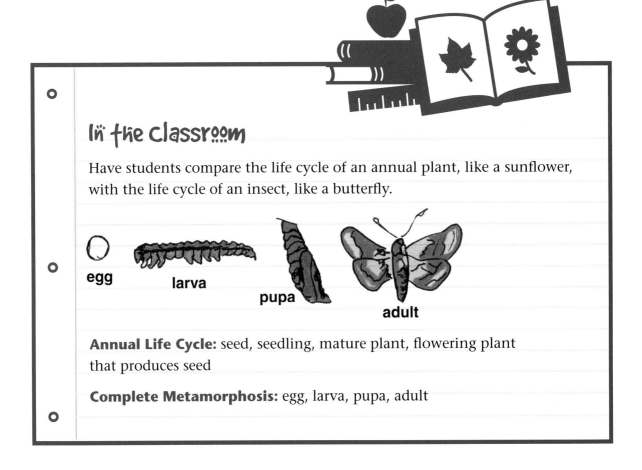

In the Classroom

Have students compare the life cycle of an annual plant, like a sunflower, with the life cycle of an insect, like a butterfly.

egg   larva   pupa   adult

Annual Life Cycle: seed, seedling, mature plant, flowering plant that produces seed

Complete Metamorphosis: egg, larva, pupa, adult

1

Have you registered your JMG group yet?

By completing the registration on pages 167–175 your group can:

- ❀ **Earn certification as a Wildlife Gardener**sm
- ❀ **Be eligible for periodic give-aways**
- ❀ **Receive the JMG National Newsletter for free**

Registering your group is **FREE** *and the National JMG Program office with send your group a free, personalized certificate recognizing your JMG Group!*

If you have any questions about registering your JMG Group, call the National Junior Master Gardener Program office at 979-845-8565 or email us at *programinfo@jmgkids.org*

Wildlife Gardener℠ Recognition Medals and Certification

Your JMGers can earn certification and recognition medals as they complete their learning as a Wildlife Gardener! Below is a description of certification and medal requirements:

Wildlife Gardener Certification

Upon completion of this Wildlife Gardener curriculum, youths in registered JMG groups can earn a Golden Ray Series certification as a Wildlife Gardener. Steps to registering a group and having youths earn a certification as a Wildlife Gardener are outlined on page XVIII. **Personalized certifications are free and are available by returning completion form available on page 175.**

Wildlife Gardener Recognition Medals

Youths can be awarded recognition medals for completing portions of Wildlife Gardener. Requirements for each of the Wildlife Gardener Recognition Medals are described below:

Wildlife Gardener Medal
Youths in registered JMG groups can be awarded a Wildlife Gardener Recognition Medal for completing any 6 activities from the Wildlife Gardener curriculum.

Service Crest Medal
Youths in registered JMG groups can be awarded a Service Crest Medal for completing a service project associated with the Wildlife Gardener curriculum. This medal is made to be fit together with the Wildlife Gardener Medal.

Golden Ray Shield

Youths in registered JMG groups completing Wildlife Gardener certification requirements can earn the Golden Ray Shield medal. The Golden Ray Shield medal is made to fit together with other Wildlife Gardener Recognition Medals and designates certification as Wildlife Gardener.

order your Wildlife Gardener Recognition Medals today by calling toll free 1-888-JMG-KIDS or online at www.jmgkids.org

Essential Elements

Teaching Concept 2

Activity 7:
Habitat Tag

(Adapted from Habitat Hunt, page 17, Schoolyard Habitats Site Planning Guide, National Wildlife Federation®)

Objective: Identify and explore components of habitat naturally existing in a given area

Time: Session One, 30 Minutes; Session Two, 30 minutes

Materials: construction paper (four colors – yellow, blue, red, green), chalkboard or poster, colored chalk or markers, string, scissors, lamp, reference materials and *Habitat Tag* worksheet (following activity)

 NOTE: This activity is complimented by P.L.A.N.T. and Wildlife Needs on page 2.

Your site may already provide adequate habitat for some animals, students may have seen squirrels romping around in nearby trees or heard songbirds in the spring. This activity may answer questions as to what these animals are finding in your schoolyard and what they and other species might lack. Identifying and locating the elements of habitat already present on school grounds represents the first step in restoring wildlife habitat.

Cut construction paper into "tags" (quarter page, rectangles) and punch a single hole in the top. Make enough so that there are four tags, one of each color to represent the elements of habitat, for every two students. Cut a 12" length of string for each card.

Habitat Hunt Tags

Yellow - Food

Blue - Water

Red - Cover

Green - Places to raise young

Session One

Review the four basic elements of habitat and the importance of each for animal survival. Have the group think of an example of each one of the elements.

2

Water such as from a ditch, a birdbath or any water feature.

Source of Food such as insects, berries, leaves, and other plant material.

Shelter that Provides Cover such as under big rocks, inside old logs and within and covered offered by plant material.

Shelter that Provides Places to Raise Young can be in shallow pools of water, dense grasses, shrubs, trees, etc.

Explain to the students that they are about to become an animal in search of a place to make a home. Tell the students that their new habitat needs to provide all of these elements.

On a chalkboard or poster board, brainstorm with the group a list of wildlife that might live in your area. Pair students together and have them each choose one of the animals from the list. Ask the group if all of the animals that were chosen have the same needs. Then ask if all of these needs are provided for in the same way. Ask if they think the element of *places to raise young* would be the same for a lizard as it is for a raccoon or a songbird. Tell the students they will be exploring an area outdoors in search of each of the elements of habitat they need to survive. Before they can look for those

elements, they need to know what those elements are.

Pass out the *Habitat Tag* worksheet. Have partners work together using field guides, reference materials, and resource links at *www.jmgkids.org/wildlifegardener* to identify the types of food, water, cover and places to raise young that their animals require. Have partners record their finds in the *Needs* column of the *Habitat Tag* worksheet.

Session Two

Once students have completed the *Needs* part of the Habitat Tag worksheet, tell them they will now go on a search to find an area that provides those needs. Define the outdoor area for the group to explore. Before going outside, review safety rules with the class and determine if students will stay together as a group, or will be allowed to investigate the school grounds on their own.

Provide set of habitat tags to each set of partners. Tell students they should tie their tags to mark the location of a habitat element for their animal. It is also a good idea to have students write the name of their species on each tag so they will be able to tell them apart from those of other wildlife and to find elements of habitat that provide for different animals.

While students are outside, have them think about the following:

- All animals need food, water, cover and a safe place to raise their young to survive.

- When outside, take a look around you. Do you see the necessary habitat elements for the animal you have chosen to survive here? Spend some time exploring this area. Look for all the characteristics of habitat that meet your specific needs. Based on what you find, decide to stay and call this area "home" or continue to look for a new place to live.

- It's possible that not all the students will find all four elements for their animals, but their challenge is to thoroughly explore the area.

- On your Habitat Tag page, describe the four elements of habitat you found that meet your needs:
  1. Food   3. Cover
  2. Water   4. Places to Raise Young

- Note where you found each element. Are they spaced close together or spread out over the area?

- Decide whether you (as the animal) would stay and set up home here. Why or why not? What other habitat elements would need to be added for you to stay here?

After they place each flag, participants will use the Habitat Tag worksheets to record what and where they found all or some of what they need to survive. While outside, be sure to help students if they feel unable to identify the elements.

Once all students are finished, tour the area together and collect the tags. Discuss the habitat elements each flag signals. Have each "animal" share what they found with the group about how the area provides for their own needs Have the class assess its findings. If possible, use a chalkboard, dry-erase board or overhead and transparency to draw a simple map of the area explored during the activity. Have each child come to the board and add the location of the elements they flagged to the map. Each element should be represented by the corresponding color of chalk (or marker). As a class, discuss the map. Which areas on the schoolyard have the most habitat elements? How many different species might each section support? Ask each student to decide if this site would be part or all of the animal's habitat. What habitat elements would need to be added to enhance or create adequate wildlife habitat?

Challenge students to think about how the availability of certain habitat elements might change through the seasons. Would water be more difficult to get for wildlife in summer or winter? Are small streams, ponds and puddles they may have seen available for wildlife all the time? What about food?

Habitat Tag

You are a _____ **and in order to survive you need food, water, cover, and places to raise young.**

List examples of what you tagged below and decide whether you'll stay and set up home here. **Good Luck and have fun!**

2

Habitat Hunt Tags

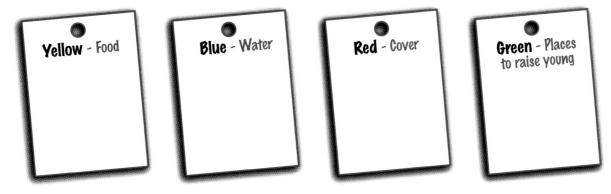

Yellow - Food

Blue - Water

Red - Cover

Green - Places to raise young

Needs

Food Source: _____

Water Source: _____

Cover: _____

Place to Raise Young: _____

Questions

Will you stay and set up home here? _____

Why or why not? _____

What would make this area a better home for you? _____

_____

Activity 8:
Shielding Shelter

Objective: Perform a dramatic interpretation of the importance of shelter for various forms of wildlife

Time: 20 Minutes

Materials: Large cardboard box, scissors, lamp or flashlight, fan and watering can with water

NOTE: Before beginning this activity, cut out an opening in the side of large box for a student to be able to crawl through. Place the box close enough to a power supply to be able to use a lamp and fan.

Ask the JMGers to raise their hands if they live under a roof. Ask the group why they think every single person in the room raised their hands. Explain that just like all people need food, water and shelter to live, animals also have these same needs.

Now ask the group to help you come up with a list of different kinds of shelters that people live in. The list will likely begin with examples such as house, apartment, duplex, etc. but also have the group think about in other parts of the world and throughout history to include examples like huts, tipis, even caves. Tell the group that all of these examples are shelters that protect people from rain, cold, heat, and wind and without that protection, we could not live. Point out that a long time ago, people had to rely

on what they could find in nature to keep them safe and that people built shelters out of items that they found. Explain that animals need two different types of shelter:

Cover – a quick shelter that protects them from predators and other dangers (such as a frog ducking under a large rock to escape from a hungry raccoon)

Place to raise young – a safe area to raise young animals (such as a bird house in a tree or dense area of shrubs for birds to nest in)

Tell the group that they are going to become animals. Ask for two volunteers to pretend to be rabbits. Be sure to involve your more animated students! Explain to the group that one of the two animals has found or made a shelter. Ask the students to imagine that the box is a shelter the rabbit has created in a hollowed out area at the base of an old rotted tree. The other rabbit does not have a shelter.

SUN and HEAT

Ask the JMGers what they would do if they were playing outside in the sun and got too hot. Shine the lamp towards the two volunteers. Ask them to pretend that the lamp is the sun. Have the group explain how each must feel. Ask one of the "rabbits" to seek shelter inside the cardboard "base of the tree". Ask if the sheltered animal would be as hot as the animal without shelter. Have the two animals act this out.

POURING RAIN

Put the "hot sun" away and have both rabbits come out of the shelter. Tell the group that the sun has gone behind the clouds and the rabbits are outdoors looking for food but now a storm is brewing. Have the sheltered rabbit again run inside. Use the watering can as rain. Walk towards the box. Raise the watering can over the box. Pour "rain" over the top of the box. Ask the volunteer in the box if he/she is wet. Walk over to the

other volunteer with the watering can. Raise the watering can over the child's head. Ask the group what would happen if it rained on this animal–and give the rabbit a light sprinkle!

COLD and WIND

Tell the group that as the rain stops, a cold front blows in. Point the fan in the direction of the two volunteers. Ask them to pretend that the fan is a very cold wind. Ask the group to tell you how each animal feels. Have the two volunteers act out the responses.

PREDATORS

Remind the group of what other reasons rabbits might need to seek shelter. Introduce the terms **predator** and **prey** to the group. Point out that shelter that provides cover to quickly protect animals is vital. Now ask for a third volunteer. This volunteer will be a predator (a wolf, a hawk, etc.). Ask the rabbit inside the shelter to come out. As the rabbits are scavenging for food this time, they are spotted by the hungry predator. The predator is hungry and is looking for food. As one of the rabbits quickly runs inside its shelter, what can the other do? Reiterate that animals, just like people, need shelter to live.

Take the group on a walk outside and explain that shelters that animals require may be very simple and very basic. Have the group look for possible places that animals might use as shelters. Ask the

group to point out any places where an animal—even some of the tiniest animals (insects)—may hide from predators or escape bad weather. JMGers might notice shelter areas they've never thought of before, such as

- Crevices along buildings

- Holes or cracks in trees

- A thick canopy of leaves

- A large shrub with dense lower foliage

- An area with tall grass

Talk with the gardeners about attracting wildlife to a garden, backyard, schoolyard, etc. Stress the importance of providing shelter for wildlife in these areas. Tell the group that they will be spending a lot of time thinking about and working to provide shelters for wildlife in the garden.

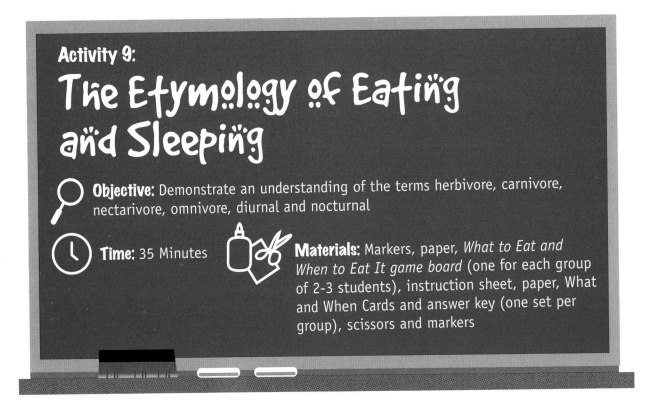

Activity 9:

The Etymology of Eating and Sleeping

Objective: Demonstrate an understanding of the terms herbivore, carnivore, nectarivore, omnivore, diurnal and nocturnal

Time: 35 Minutes

Materials: Markers, paper, *What to Eat and When to Eat It game board* (one for each group of 2-3 students), instruction sheet, paper, What and When Cards and answer key (one set per group), scissors and markers

Ask the group if they have ever wondered where a word comes from. That is what etymology is all about—word origins.

Write "vore" on a chalkboard or poster. Tell the gardeners that "vore" is a word part that means "to eat." Write "herbi" on another poster or sheet of paper. Explain that this word part means "plants." Place the "herbi" word to the left of the "vore"

word. Ask the group to tell you what they think the word **herbivore** means. Ask everyone to think of some animals that they think might fit this description (rabbits, deer, squirrels). Repeat the process with the word **carnivore** (wolves, cats, snakes) in which "carni" means meat.

Ask if anyone knows what category human beings fit into. Ask the group

A **nectarivore** is an animal or insect that largely consumes nectar for its nourishment such as many butterflies, hummingbirds, and bees.

if people like to eat hamburgers. Have the group tell you what items may be found on a hamburger as an example that people eat both plants and meat.

Draw two overlapping circles to create a Venn diagram (see below) on another poster and write herbivore in one circle and carnivore in the other:

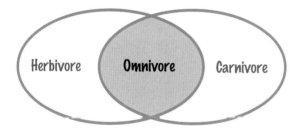

Venn diagrams are made up of two overlapping circles in which shared characteristics can be represented in the overlapping area.

Write "omni" on another piece of paper and place it to the left of "vore". Explain that "omni" means "all." Omnivores eat everything—plants and meat! Write the terms within the diagram as shown above. Ask the group to think of some examples of animals that they might see in their area and write them within the correct place in the diagram. If a student thinks of an animal and the group is not sure where it should be placed, write it to the side with a question mark for later research.

Tell the group that they have just learned words that can let a person know what an animal might eat. Explain that over time animals have adapted to be very successful at finding food during certain times of the day. It's important for them to learn two more words that will let them know when an animal will eat and/or be active.

Write the word **diurnal** on a poster board or sheet of paper. Explain that "dia" comes from the Latin word meaning "by day." A **diurnal** animal eats and is active during the day. Ask the group

Herbivore

Mouse   Deer   Rabbit
Moose   Beaver   Groundhog

omnivore

Racoon   Bear   Turtle
People   Squirrel   Fox

Carnivore

Wolf   Hawk   Snake
Frog   Weasel   Spider

Crepuscular describes animals that are active during the twilight times at dusk and dawn.

to give some examples (birds, butterflies, squirrels).

Write the word **nocturnal** on a poster board or sheet of paper. Explain that "noctu" come from the Latin word meaning "from the night." A **nocturnal** animal eats and is active during the night. Ask for some examples of nocturnal animals (owls, raccoons, mice).

Have the group play the "What to Eat and When to Eat It" game by dividing the group into smaller groups of 2-3 students.

Copy and assemble the What and When to Eat game board from the appendix and copy a set of What and When Cards and answer key per group. Explain the rules and how to play the game. Have each person find a small stone, coin or other item to be used as a game piece. Place each game piece on the "start square." Select who goes first for each group.

What to Eat and When to Eat It Game

How to Play

1. Place the game board on a flat surface. Shuffle the What and When Cards and place them face down near the game board. Place your game pieces on the Start Square.

2. The first person picks an What and When Cards. She reads the card and follows the instructions.

3. The second person then picks a card, reads it and follows the instructions.

4. Continue picking cards until someone reaches the last square on the game board. When you have used all of the cards, shuffle them so you can use them again.

What to Eat and When to Eat It Rules

1. No peeking at the Answer Key!

2. Players pick one What and When Cards per turn.

3. Players can challenge other players. If a player thinks that another player has made a mistake, he can challenge that player after she has finished with her turn. To challenge another player, say, "What to Eat and When to Eat Challenge!" Look at the answer key to determine the correct answer. If the other player has made a mistake, she must move her game piece back to where it was and she does not get to pick another card. If the player's move was correct, the challenger loses his next turn.

4. The winner is the first player to reach the finish section!

Answer Key

A diurnal animal would be active:
During the day

A nocturnal animal would be active:
During the night

Herbivores

 This squirrel is an herbivore and can eat:pinecones, nuts, and berries.

This rabbit is an herbivore and can eat:plants and garden fruits/vegetables.

 This deer is an herbivore and can eat: Small plants, leaves and twigs of some shrubs and trees, acorns, berries, apples, corn

This raccoon is an omnivores and can eat: Small animals(salamanders, mice, fish, birds, frogs, insects), bird eggs, plants including berries and other garden fruits/vegetables.

These people are omnivores and on this gameboard might eat: Animals (fish, rabbit, deer, crab), eggs, berries, seeds and other garden fruits/vegetables

Carnivores

 This snake is a carnivore and can eat: Insects, eggs, other small animals (such as mice, small rabbits, frogs, salamanders, birds, fish)

omnivores

 This mouse is an omnivore and can eat: Seeds, fruit, berries, and insects

Nectarivores

 This hummingbird is a nectarivore and can eat: From flowers

This butterfly is a nectarivore and can eat: From flowers

What and When Cards

Rabbit

You are an **herbivore.**

Move to the closest space that has a picture of something you would eat.

Raccoon

You are an **omnivore.**

Move to the closest space that has a picture of something you would eat.

Snake

You are a **carnivore.**

Move to the closest space that has a picture of something you would eat.

Butterfly

You are a **nectarivore.**

Move to the closest space that has a picture of something you would eat.

Person

You are an omnivore.

Move to the closest space that has a picture of something you would eat.

Deer

You are an herbivore.

Move to the closest space that has a picture of something you would eat.

Hummingbird

You are a nectarivore.

Move to the closest space that has a picture of something you would eat.

Squirrel

You are an herbivore.

Move to the closest space that has a picture of something you would eat.

Mouse

You are **nocturnal**.

Move to the closest space that has a picture of when you are active.

Butterfly

You are **diurnal**.

Move to the closest space that has a picture of when you are active.

Bat

You are **nocturnal**.

Move to the closest space that has a picture of when you are active.

Eastern Grey Squirrel

You are **diurnal**.

Move to the closest space that has a picture of when you are active.

Raccoon
You are **nocturnal.**

Move to the closest space
that has a picture of when
you are active.

Songbird
You are **diurnal.**

Move to the closest space
that has a picture of when
you are active.

2

Your wildlife has become
the prey of another animal.

Go Back to
the Start

There is no longer a
habitat nearby.

Go Back to
the Start

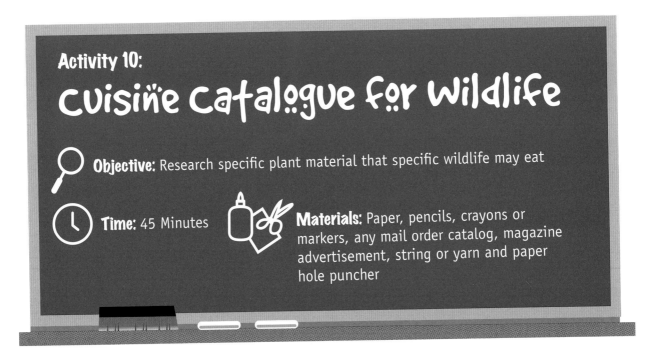

Activity 10:

Cuisine Catalogue for Wildlife

Objective: Research specific plant material that specific wildlife may eat

Time: 45 Minutes

Materials: Paper, pencils, crayons or markers, any mail order catalog, magazine advertisement, string or yarn and paper hole puncher

Ask the gardeners if they like to watch TV. Ask them if they have ever seen a commercial that made them want to buy a certain toy or food. Show the group a magazine ad showing a particularly popular or tasty-looking food. Explain that the purpose of an advertisement in a magazine, newspaper, or catalogue is the same as a commercial they might see on TV—to get people to buy the product. Show the gardeners examples of mail order catalogs. Point out that most ads make products more attractive by including mixture of facts about the product (Contains all natural ingredients!) as well as opinions (New and improved taste!). Have students locate examples of both facts and opinions in the sample catalog ads.

Tell the group that they are going to use some of the ideas they see in these ads to create their own catalog food advertisement to make a certain type of plant attractive to an certain animal. They will then put all of the group's ads together to create a unique catalog—a catalog for wildlife. Their catalog will be filled with advertisements for food that certain wildlife may want to eat.

Divide the class into small groups of 2-3. Each group will need a piece of paper (punch holes in the margins of the papers), pencils, and crayons or markers. Ask each group to choose an animal from the list on the next page or some other species of local wildlife. Each group should research using reference materials or online resources links available at *www.jmgkids.org/wildlifegardener* to find one type of food that their chosen animal may want to eat. (Duplicates of animals are OK as long as a different food type is chosen.) Tell the groups that they are going to design an advertisement for the food type that they chose. Their ads should attract the animal they picked and should be very "eye-catching" and enticing, similar to those in a mail-order catalog or other advertisement. The groups should include the following when designing their ads:

- A drawing or photo of the product

- A written description

- Location where to find the food

Allow each group to present their ads to the class or large group. Students should use their ads, information they learned and props to create a 15-second commercial that teaches what they know about their plant selection and then perform it. Commercials can be in the form of an announcer sharing the information or even better, students could create a memorable slogan, jingle or even a brief skit to feature their wildlife-attracting plant.

After all the groups have finished, bind their advertisements by stapling or stringing together to make a catalog. As the group begins making decision about plants that might be brought into the garden habitat, the research and information of plants *Cuisine Catalogue for Wildlife*, can be a valuable resource.

Plants native to your area would be an ideal to feature within your group's Cuisine Catalogue for Wildlife! Contact your local county Extension office or visit links available at www.jmgkids.org/wildlifegardener for more information about native plants in your area.

Suggested Wildlife and Catalogue Cuisine

Bees: many flowers

Butterflies: flowers, rotting fruit

Caterpillars: leaves, stems

Hummingbirds: many flowers

Songbirds: seeds, fruit (includes nuts)

Squirrels: fruit (includes nuts), seeds, stems

Turtles: fruit, mushrooms, leaves, stems
(only some species of turtles are plant eaters)

Rabbits: leaves, bark, twigs

In the Classroom

The written description can be a good way to introduce descriptive and persuasive forms of writing. Have students team up for a brief writing workshop in which they share ideas for finding words that are particularly descriptive and appealing. Once students have researched their animal and decided on a plant, have each write one sentence to describe the featured plant. Arrange class so that there are at least four on each writing team. Each student should have their paper with their sentence and a pencil. Have students pass their papers to the right. Set a timer for 60 seconds. The student's should read the sentence on the paper passed to them, think about it for a few seconds and then add any new adjectives or descriptive phrases that come to mind. When the minute is up, the students pass the paper again so that each person in the team sees each others paper for one minute. When these writing brainstorms are over, the original groups can share all of the ideas that were suggested and decide which sentences to include.

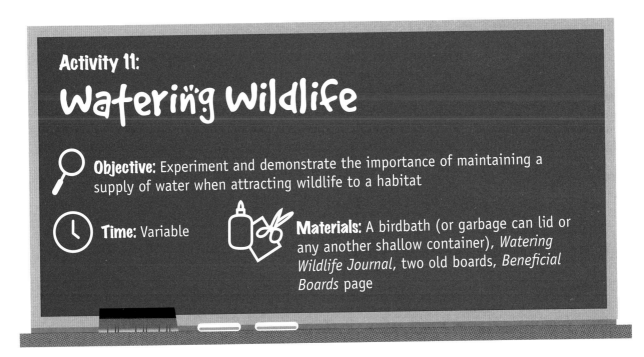

Activity 11:
Watering Wildlife

Objective: Experiment and demonstrate the importance of maintaining a supply of water when attracting wildlife to a habitat

Time: Variable

Materials: A birdbath (or garbage can lid or any another shallow container), *Watering Wildlife Journal*, two old boards, *Beneficial Boards* page

2

A habitat for wildlife is an area that provides all of the basics an animal needs to live. One of the most important features of a habitat is a water source. Complete both parts of this activity to help your gardeners provide a source of moisture for wildlife.

Part 1

Ask the JMGers the following questions:

1. Have you ever been playing outside and became really thirsty?

2. Were you able to get a drink? From where?

Explain to the group that it is important for wildlife to find places to drink. Ask the group if an area without a water source can be a suitable habitat for wildlife. Explain that even though animals don't have access to a water faucet for moisture, water is a renewable resource

and animals have always been able to get it from water that falls from the sky and naturally collects in lakes rivers, ditches and even puddles! Water is component of habitat that all living things in the world need to survive and animals will seek it out. If you plan on attracting wildlife to your backyard, schoolyard or local park, it is necessary to provide water for the animals. Over time this type of set-up will most likely attract many types of small animals.

Place a birdbath, garbage can lid, or another large shallow container in an area where the group would like to attract wildlife. Fill the container with water. Have the group hypothesize about what will happen with the water sources. Will the sources attract any wildlife? How long might it take for birds or any other wildlife to find the source of water? After a few days, periodically take the group back to the area (standing a distance away from it) to observe. Have the group make observations anytime they are walking by the area. Even if wildlife are not present at a given time, have the group examine the water source and area around it for evidence wildlife may have visited the area. Have the group record their observations on their *Watering Wildlife Journal* on three separate visits to the site.

Note that in some cases, it may take a few days for wildlife to find the water source. Periodically have the group observe this area to see what happens over time and to clean and refill the water source every few days.

Part 2

Water and moisture can also attract smaller creatures like spiders, earthworms, beetles, and pillbugs. Many of these wildlife are beneficial to a garden setting. For example, a lot of the smaller creatures are good at making compost. Spiders can help in our gardens by catching unwanted insects. Some of these tiny wildlife also serve as prey of other animals the JMGers might want to attract to the garden (like frogs or birds). Tell the group that they are going to also try to attract some of these beneficial creatures and other insects to their wildlife garden area.

Gather two boards. They can be any type of board, such as old fence pickets or scrap pieces of wood from a construction site. Place one of the two boards on the ground in a sunny, dry place. Place the second board in a shady area and cover lightly with a layer of leaves or grass. The gardeners should keep the area around the second board moist (but not soggy). Have the group make predictions about what they think will happen. Will either board attract anything? How long will it take any wildlife to find them? What type of wildlife will the boards attract?

After a few days, observe what has happened. Lift the first board and ask the group to record what they see on their *Beneficial Boards* pages. Do the same for the second board. Have the group give their ideas of why there was little if any wildlife under the dry board.

Both of these activities provide a source of moisture in a wildlife garden. Explain that the longer a source of water is in an area, the more likely wildlife will make the area a part of their habitat.

In the Classroom

Ask the gardeners to choose one of the animals they observed visiting their water source or under one of their boards. Ask them to write a story about it from the *animal's* point of view. Allow students time to research and familiarize themselves with the wildlife and determine its "personality." For example, a reclusive animals may have a shy personality and be skittish, whereas an intelligent animal, such as a raccoon, may be confident and clever with a sense of humor! If possible have a dramatic reading from each of the animals. Below is a sample of a student's writing describing a day in the life of a pillbug.

"It was one of those days where everything goes wrong. I was curled up in a little ball sleeping when all of the sudden I heard a rumbling sound and the ground started shaking. They were mowing again! I was running as fast as I could go when I felt two big human fingers grab me. It was a kindergartener! I rolled up in a ball to protect myself and the kid started rolling me around like a marble on the hot sidewalk. I rolled off into the grass. I looked up and saw a big board lying on the ground. I ran quickly under it to hide. I was very safe and cool AND there were water drops all over the place! I was thirsty and I drank a half of a water drop without even taking a breath! Since it was so cool and dark and my stomach was full, I decided to roll up back into a ball and go back to sleep."

Watering Wildlife Journal

observation 1:

How many days has the water source been in place? _____

Do you see any wildlife? _____

If so, what types? _____

Any evidence wildlife has visited the area? _____

_____

observation 2:

How many days has the water source been in place? _____

Do you see any wildlife? _____

If so, what types? _____

Any evidence wildlife has visited the area? _____

_____

observation 3:

How many days has the water source been in place? _____

Do you see any wildlife? _____

If so, what types? _____

Any evidence wildlife has visited the area? _____

_____

Did you see more and more wildlife the longer water was available? _____

Why do you think this happened? _____

How many different types of wildlife did you attract by providing water? _____

_____

Beneficial Boards

Which board do you think will attract the most wildlife? _____

Why do you think this will happened? _____

Which board do you think will attract the most wildlife? _____

Why do you think this will happen? _____

Board in sunny dry area:

Do you see any wildlife? _____

What types of wildlife are present? _____

How many of each species of wildlife are present? _____

_____

_____

_____

How many of them would be beneficial to have in a garden? _____

Board in shady, moist area:

Do you see any wildlife? _____

What types of wildlife are present? _____

How many of each species of wildlife are present? _____

_____

_____

_____

How many of them would be beneficial to have in a garden? _____

Which board attracted the most wildlife? _____

Why do you think this happened? _____

_____

Activity 12:
Design-a-Dwelling

Objective: Develop a creative design that meets the need for shelter for wildlife survival

Time: 30 Minutes

Materials: Paper, pens, pencils and markers

Ask the group if they have the same needs as the wildlife they are learning about. Do the habitats we all live within have any similarities to wildlife? Review the needs represented by the four components of habitat:

• Water

• Source of Food

• Shelter that Provides Cover

• Shelter that Provides Places to Raise Young

Point out that although our examples of these components are different, people do require those same components of food, water, and shelter. Have the gardeners think specifically about their homes and discuss the following questions:

1. What do you like the most about your house?

2. What do you not like about it?

3. How does it keep you warm when it is cold outside?

4. How does it keep you cool when it is hot outside?

5. How does it keep you dry when it rains?

6. Is it big enough for you and your family? Too small? Just right?

7. What different rooms make up your home? (On a chalkboard or poster create a map of your home.)

8. If you could live in a perfect house, how would be different from your house?

Tell the gardeners that they are going to design the perfect house, but this perfect home will be for a bird. Discuss specific reasons why a bird needs a home. Be sure to talk about protection from the elements, shelter from predators, and protection for eggs. Ask the group to pretend that they are birds. What type of house would they want? What types of things would be useful for a bird to have in its house? Divide the class into groups of 2-3 and give them a few minutes to brainstorm and create a list of the features that the perfect dwelling for a bird would include. If the groups come to the conclusion that the perfect dwelling would depend on the species of bird, have them select what bird would be living in their dwelling.

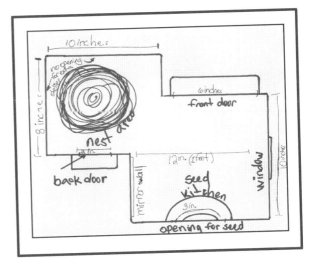

Give each student a piece of paper, pencil, and markers or crayons. Ask everyone to create a sketch to map the design their perfect birdhouse that they would live in if they were birds. Encourage them to first create a rough sketch to form their plan then to a finish by making a neater, more detailed map. The map should include labels for each room, openings to the house and any other amenities.

Allow time for each student to share their created homes with the rest of the group. When the students have finished, review the components of habitat and ask them to point out those components available just in the dwellings they've created.

If possible, consider the feasibility of constructing one of the designed dwellings to create and add to your habitat garden area. Whether choosing one of the drawings randomly or having students vote, consider the possibility of pulling in a crafty parent, a shop class at a local high school or have your own class actually build the perfect birdhouse!

In the Classroom

After the drawings are completed, tell the group that they are going to show off their houses as if they were trying to sell them to birds. Show the group the real estate section of a local newspaper. Read a brief description of one of the houses for sale. Have each person write her own real estate listing for her birdhouse.

Double level home in the sky!

Located high above a family's backyard atop a 15 foot pole. Includes a room to hold insects and keep your extra seed dry. Don't miss this spacious birdhouse – a perfect 21st century nest for your family.

Wildlife:
Birds

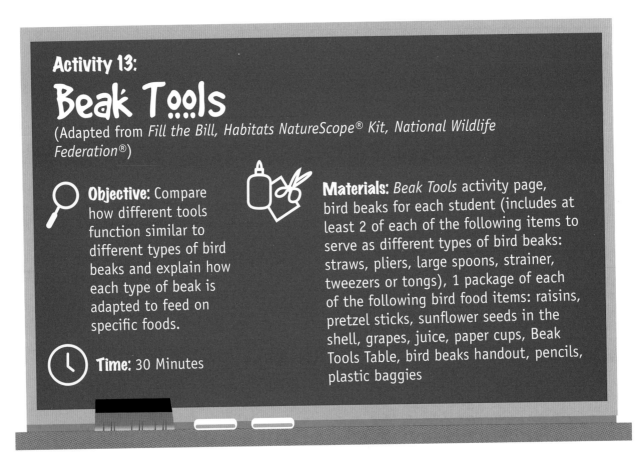

Activity 13:

Beak Tools

(Adapted from *Fill the Bill, Habitats NatureScope® Kit, National Wildlife Federation®*)

Objective: Compare how different tools function similar to different types of bird beaks and explain how each type of beak is adapted to feed on specific foods.

Time: 30 Minutes

Materials: *Beak Tools* activity page, bird beaks for each student (includes at least 2 of each of the following items to serve as different types of bird beaks: straws, pliers, large spoons, strainer, tweezers or tongs), 1 package of each of the following bird food items: raisins, pretzel sticks, sunflower seeds in the shell, grapes, juice, paper cups, Beak Tools Table, bird beaks handout, pencils, plastic baggies

Ask the JMGers if all people like the same types of food. Have some group members share what their favorite foods are. Point out to the group that not everyone eats the same foods. Similarly, not all animals eat the same types of food.

Ask the group to imagine a hummingbird trying to gobble up a mouse or a hawk trying to fit its large beak and short tongue into a flower to slurp up nectar. Explain that different bird species have beaks and tongues adapted to eating a certain type of food. Some birds have beaks good for tearing and others can use their beak to crack open hard nut shells.

Pass out handout (or show links with pictures of different types of beaks at *www.jmgkids.org/wildlifegardener*) showing different bird beaks to students. Ask students what they notice about the shapes of the beaks. Are they all the same? What do birds do with their beaks? How does the beak help birds survive? Talk about some of the examples of different bird beaks discussed above.

Divide the class into smaller groups of five. Each person in each group will have a different type of beak. Give each child in each group one of the following tools:

- Drinking straw
- pliers
- 2 large spoons
- strainer
- tweezers or tongs

Scatter all the food items over a large table or grouping of desks. Explain that they can pick up food only with their beaks and drop the food into the plastic baggies; they cannot use their hands to touch the food. Instruct students to pick up as many objects as they can in 30 seconds, using only their given tool. Time the students and have them count up the different types of objects and record that numbers on the *Beak Tool* activity page.

Replenish the desks with a few more of each of the food items. Have students switch tools with one another so they all have a different tool this round. Provide a fresh straw and cup of juice for each session! Repeat the 30-second activity. Have students count up their objects again. What did they discover about their tools? Discuss the benefits and disadvantages of each tool in picking up different foods.

3

Hummingbirds have long beaks and tongues to probe flowers for nectar. The beak protects the tongue, which slurps the nectar.

Curlews, godwits, kiwis and snipes have very long beaks to probe for worms, crustaceans and other small creatures in mud and water.

Cardinals, sparrows, grosbeaks and other finch-like birds have very short, cone-shaped beaks. These beaks are very strong and can break open tough seeds.

Spoonbills and pelicans have long, flattened or pouch-like beaks that they use to scoop up fish and other aquatic creatures.

Flamingos and some ducks have bills that act like strainers to filter tiny plants and animals from the water. (Only certain kinds of ducks are filter feeders.)

Nighthawks, whip-poor-wills, swifts and swallows have large gaping mouths that act like nets to trap insects. These birds catch insects flying through the air.

Warblers have small, sharp, pointed beaks for picking insects from leaves, logs and twigs.

Toucans have very long, thick beaks for reaching out and plucking fruit from trees.

47

Afterwards, ask students how the tools they used relate to real bird beaks pictured on the handout. Do any have similar shapes? Discuss this with students before having them match the tools with the beaks on the handout. Above each bird picture on the handout, have students write the letter of the tool that best matches the beak. Ask students, What do you think would happen to a bird that ate nectar if it had the beak of a cardinal (which eats seeds)? Would it be able to survive? Have students also make a hypothesis about what each bird actually eats and write it next to the bird. If possible, allow students time to investigate answers to their questions by researching reference materials or visiting resource links at: *www.jmgkids.org/wildlifegardener*.

Explain that many birds have adapted to have very specialized beaks. The beaks allow the birds to eat a certain kind of food. Ask students how they think a specialized beak helps birds survive. (A bird with a specialized beak may be able to eat a type of food that no other bird can eat.) Could they imagine a situation in which it might actually harm the bird to have such a specialized beak? (If the bird's habitat changes and its food is no longer available, the bird might die because it can't eat anything else.)

Remind the group that if they want to encourage certain birds to their garden, they will need to make sure that they are providing a food source that those bird can access.

Not all birds have such specialized beaks. Crows, for example, can use their beaks to eat a variety of foods, like fruits, nuts, berries, dead animals, fish and small rodents. Crows are generalists, and if one type of food is not available they can easily eat something else.

In the Classroom

Ask everyone to think about what type of beaks they would like to have if they were birds. Ask them to think about how the design of a beak affects what a bird can eat, just as they saw in the Beak Tools game that they played. Explain to the group that each one of them is going to design their own bird beak. Some students might choose a multipurpose beak. Have each person draw a picture of her beak. Or ask everyone to create a model of her bird beaks with arts and crafts supplies. After everyone is finished, have the JMGers take turns explaining to the group how the beaks work and what they can be used for.

3

Beak Tools

Think about how are birds adapted for eating different kids of food.

1. **Circle the tool you used and write how many of each food item you were able to pick up.**

2. **Match the letter of the following tools with the bird beaks below.**

A. Straw
___ raisins ___ grapes ___ pretzels ___ sunflower seeds ___ juice

B. Nutcracker or Pliers
___ raisins ___ grapes ___ pretzels ___ sunflower seeds ___ juice

C. Large Spoons
___ raisins ___ grapes ___ pretzels ___ sunflower seeds ___ juice

D. Strainer
___ raisins ___ grapes ___ pretzels ___ sunflower seeds ___ juice

E. Tweezers or Tongs
___ raisins ___ grapes ___ pretzels ___ sunflower seeds ___ juice

Think of something else each food item below could represent and write them in the blanks below.

_____ raisins _____ grapes _____ pretzels

_____ sunflower seeds _____ juice

Write the letter from the tools above that you think best matches the bird beaks below.

_____ _____ _____ _____ _____

Hummingbird   **Grosbeck**   **Flamingo**   **Pelican**   **Snipe**

_____ _____ _____ _____ _____

Based on its beak, what do you think each bird might eat in the wild?
Write your hypothesis below each bird on the line above.

50

Activity 14:
Name That Tune

Objective: Investigate how birds communicate and identify birds by their songs and calls

Time: Variable

Materials: Internet access, tape recorder, Name That Tune Worksheet, paper and pencils

NOTE - Before beginning this activity, familiarize yourself with websites that offer libraries of songs or calls from birds found in your area. These resource links can be found at www.jmgkids.org/wildlifegardener

Have the group listen to several of the songs you chose that are common to your area. Point out that one of the benefits of having birds in the garden is being able to enjoy hearing the bird songs and calls. Play each of the songs 3-4 times and as students are trying to become familiar with each of the sounds, invite them to try to mimic the song each time you play it. Have the group note differences and similarities between the songs.

Now randomly play each of the songs the group has listened to. Challenge the group to try to identify one of the songs you played just by its sound.

Tell the group that many people can identify birds by their songs rather than by seeing them. Take the group outdoors. First, have the group sit and listen for one

minute. Then have students spend one minute trying to mimic the bird sounds they practiced indoors. After the group stops, ask them to listen and watch. Did they notice any more or less movement of birds? Did they hear more or fewer, or different bird sounds afterwards?

Take the group on a short walk through an area were birds may be present. Whether it is outside in the immediate area or though a park area, have the group listen for sounds of birds calling. If possible, have the group record bird songs they hear. As the group is listening, have the students make notes on their *Name That Tune* Worksheets.

If the group is able to record any bird songs, have them go back inside and listen to the songs. Have the group work to identify each song and record this information on the *Name That Tune* Worksheet. First, have the group decide if each of the songs is one of the several they heard before going outdoors. If its not, challenge the group to access the resource links at *www.jmgkids.org/wildlifegardener* to discover the mystery song bird.

You can also extend the activity by breaking the group into smaller groups of 3 –5 "bird" bands.. Each member of the group should try to "master" one of the bird songs they've heard. Each individual's bird sound will serve as an "instrument" of the band. Each group of students should create a name of their group's band and begin working

on a performance. This performance can include the different bird sounds performed together, in a certain order or in anyway that the group decides is fun. Give the groups a range of 30-60 seconds that the performance should last.

If time allows, have the bands create costumes by cutting out feather shapes, wing shapes, and/or beak shapes from construction paper or other art supplies. Once each group has created a song and practiced their performance of it, have a Battle of the Bird Bands. Ask each group to perform their song in front of the other groups. You may want to invite parents, friends, etc. to attend the Battle of the Bird Bands!

What's the difference between a bird call and a bird song? What are their purposes?

Songs and calls are both inherited and learned characteristics that serve to help birds survive and reproduce. Songs are usually given by adult males on their territory during the nesting season. Calls are simpler bird sounds that occur throughout the year to

- **Express alarm**
- **Maintain contact with other members of a flock**
- **Interact with a mate or young bird**

In the Classroom

Choose a bird song or call of a bird that is seen in your area and play it for the students. Ask them to describe the sound. Tell the group that scientists sometimes try to describe bird calls and songs by spelling them. Play the song or call for the group again. Ask the class to try to create a sound spelling of what they hear. You will likely need to play it several more times. Have volunteers share the phonetic spelling they have created to represent the sounds and have them perform it. Students can listen and vote to determine which spelling best represents the sound.

Choose several more local songs or calls for the group to "translate." Divide students into groups of 2-3 and have them work together to create a phonetic spelling for each song or call. Play each one several times as they work to create the spelling and once the class is finished, have them vote again for the most accurate spelling of each.

Next, have the groups listen again to the songs one by one and have them time try to create words or a phrase of what it sounds like the bird is "saying." This creation of a word or phrase to be able to repeat and remember what the sound sounds like is called a mnemonic.

Visit the resource links at _www.jmgkids.org/wildlifegardener_ and compare their work with examples of both bird phonetics and mnemonics. Next have the class create a "Bird Songs and Calls of Our Community" booklet and as time is available, use it to teach younger students or other groups to identify and mimic bird sounds.

Name That Tune Worksheet

Song # _____

What time of day was this song recorded? _____

Where was this song recorded? _____

If you saw this bird, what did it look like? _____

_____

Describe the song. _____

_____

What kind of bird produced this song? _____

Song # _____

What time of day was this song recorded? _____

Where was this song recorded? _____

If you saw this bird, what did it look like? _____

_____

Describe the song. _____

_____

What kind of bird produced this song? _____

Activity 15:
Far-out Feeders

Objective: Use various household materials to create bird feeders, utilize various types of bird feeder types and determine their effectiveness

Time: Variable

Materials: Depends on feeder types. See instructions on pages 57-58.

3

 NOTE - most of these feeders will require adult help and/or supervision.
CAUTION! Be sure to replace wet birdseed often and periodically wash bird feeders.

Ask the JMGers to tell you where they usually eat supper. Explain that not everyone eats in the same surroundings. Some people like to eat in a kitchen, while others prefer a more formal dining room setting. Birds, too, have preferences about where they eat. Some birds like to eat from a feeder suspended in the air. Some like to eat from feeders attached to tree trunks. And, some birds like to eat from flat surfaces close to the ground.

Tell the group that they are going to build various types of bird feeders and find out if some feeders attract more birds than others do. They may also discover that certain birds prefer to use certain types of feeders.

Have the group make at least two of the feeders listed on the next page. You may decide to assign one feeder type per group. Or, if time permits and the group is large enough, try all four feeders!

Using a bottle with a metal cap, a small nail, and a couple of coat hangers, JMGers can make a recycled hummingbird feeder!

After the feeders have been in place for several days, take the group outside to observe. Continue to observe over the next few weeks. Ask the group the following questions:

1. Did certain kinds of birds prefer certain types of feeders?

2. What types of birds did each feeder type attract?

3. What type of feeder(s) attracted the most birds? Why?

4. What types of feeder(s) attracted the least amount of birds? Why?

Point out to the group that certain birds are more prevalent during certain parts of the year and may be active only at certain times of the day. Have the group visit *www.jmgkids.org/wildlifegardener* to learn more about these birds and when they are more likely to be in your area. Encourage JMGers to refill the feeders regularly and visit the feeders at different times of day to monitor their use.

In the Classroom

Have the students use their observation skills and creativity to design a new kind of Far-Out Feeder made from recycled materials! They should first decide on the type of feeder they want to create and look for any type of safe materials that could be reused, recycled, or adapted to serve as an effective, even attractive feeder. The students can sketch their design, create a diagram complete with measurements and dimensions, and write a brief how-to description that provides instructions on how to build it!

See information about the *Far-Out Feeder Gallery* at the end of this activity.

Far-out Feeder Gallery

Type I: Hanging Feeders

Orange Feeder

Materials: one orange or grapefruit, spoon, peanut butter, string or wire, birdseed

Cut the orange or grapefuit in half. Scoop out most of the flesh and seeds leaving the peel (or rind) intact. Spread a layer of peanut butter over the inside of the scooped out fruit.

Punch one hole in one side of the orange near the top (open side). Punch a second hole across from the first. These two holes will be used for hanging the feeder. Tie string or wrap wire through the two holes to create the hanger. Fill the orange with birdseed and hang from the limb of a tree or under a building eave.

Milk Jug Feeder

Materials: washed milk jug, nail, scissors, string or wire, paint or markers, birdseed

Punch a hole near the spout of a milk jug using the point of a nail. Next, make a second hole across from the first. Tie string or wire through the holes to create a hanger. Cut a half circle shape out of three sides of the milk jug, excluding the handle side. These are the openings where the birds can access the seeds. Decorate the milk jug with paint or markers. Fill with seed and hang outside.

Hint: Sunflower seed will help attract more songbirds.

Type II: Raised Platform Feeders

Board Feeder

Materials: wooden board, bricks, birdseed

Place a board on a few bricks so that the board is stable and slightly raised off the ground. Scatter birdseed on the board. Replace seeds if they become wet. Or, place the board securely in a low fork of a tree. Or, scatter seeds on a tree stump.

Type III: Hummingbird Feeder

Recycled Bottle and Wire Hummingbird Feeder

Materials: Bottle with screw-on metal lid (rinsed well), small nail and hammer, wire coat hangar (or other heavy gauge wire), water, sugar, string

Using a hammer and small nail, tap a pin hole-sized opening in the center of the metal cap. Use paint pens to decorate the cap to resemble a blooming flower. Be sure to use the color red! Show your group how to use coat hanger to create a "harness" for the bottle. Dissolve 1/4 cup of sugar into 1 cup of hot water. After the sugar water has cooled, pour the mixture inside the bottle. Hang feeders with openings pointed down in the garden area.

NOTE: When the bottle is first turned upside down, the mixture will leak for several seconds until the pressure lowers enough to hold the liquid inside.

Let us know your creative ideas for feeding your feathered friends! Send a description of your feeder and tell us how you made it and how you got the idea along with a picture of your Far Out Feeder. Selected feeders will be posted at the Far Out Feeder Gallery at the JMG Website!

For info on submitting your idea go to: *www.jmgkids.org/wildlifegardener*

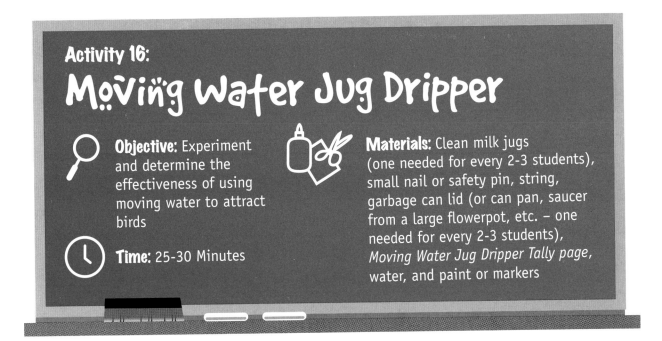

Activity 16:
Moving Water Jug Dripper

Objective: Experiment and determine the effectiveness of using moving water to attract birds

Time: 25-30 Minutes

Materials: Clean milk jugs (one needed for every 2-3 students), small nail or safety pin, string, garbage can lid (or can pan, saucer from a large flowerpot, etc. – one needed for every 2-3 students), *Moving Water Jug Dripper Tally page*, water, and paint or markers

Tell the group that although water in a habitat can attract birds, many people believe that movement of water or even the sound of moving water is more effective at drawing birds to an area. Tell the group that they will test this idea using water and recycling a milk jug to make a Moving Water Jug Dripper.

Divide students into groups of 2-3. Each group will work to create their own dripper. After discussing the importance of being careful and reviewing the safety rules, show the students how to use the point of a small nail or safety pin to punch one tiny hole at the bottom of each milk jug. The hole should be just large enough for water to slowly drip through. Then punch a larger hole in the lid to allow air in. Have the gardeners decorate their jug with paint or markers. Have students find an area that the Moving Water Jug Drippers can be located and help them hang their jugs 1-2 feet above the pan using a string tied around the handle and looped over a tree branch. Students should then fill the milk jug with water and let the dripping begin. If the hole is small enough, the water will drip over a period of 1-2 hours and can be refilled a few times a day. Have the students create a schedule to refill the jug drippers.

Experiment to see if moving water is more attractive than water that is stationary by having the group place several pans of still water grouped together in another part of the area. After the water has been in place for several days, have JMGers begin observing the areas and recording each sighting with a tally mark on the *Moving Water Jug Dripper Tally* page.

Tell the group that they have recreated what many bird would have access to in nature – moving water that might come in the form of a flowing creek or light rain showers. Share with the group that if birds had access to still water only, that water might become stagnant and be unhealthy for them. Many people believe that the moving water and the sound of it moving is attractive to birds because moving water occurring in nature is likely to be cleaner and healthier for them!

This activity can also be assigned as homework. Have the students regularly refill the jug when needed and record tallies of birds spotted over a few days. You can also have the group recreate the experiment in another location that is more or less shaded or isolated or nearer or farther to a planted area, to see if results vary. Explain to the students that the more times an experiment is repeated, the better the chances the experiment really does show what they are trying to find.

In the Classroom

Exactly how long does a moving jug dripper drip? How fast does it drip? Have students find out by determining the exact volume that is being placed in the container to begin the experiment and exactly how many minutes it takes for the jug to empty. Once you have those numbers, have students help determine the rate for periods of time. For example, if it takes about 90 minutes for 1 gallon of water to empty, it takes about 45 minute for two quarts to drip and so forth.

90 minutes   1 gallon

45 minutes   2 quarts

22 minutes   1 quart

11 minutes   1 pint

5 minutes   2 cups

2 minutes   1 cup

1 minute   ½ cup

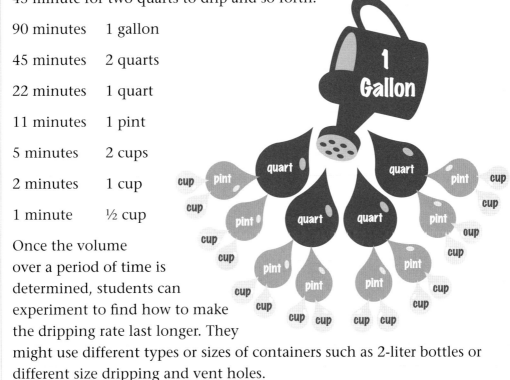

Once the volume over a period of time is determined, students can experiment to find how to make the dripping rate last longer. They might use different types or sizes of containers such as 2-liter bottles or different size dripping and vent holes.

Moving Water Jug Dripper Tally

Name:_____

Which do you think will be more attractive to birds?

_____ stationary water

_____ moving water

Why do you think that?

_____

_____

How many total jug drippers are being used?_____

_____

How many pans of stationary water are being used?_____

Over the next several days and at different times during the day, check the pans of water and make a tally mark for each bird you see:

Moving Water Jug Dripper Tally _____

Stationary Water Tally _____

Was there a difference in the number of birds visiting the two forms of water? _____

Why do you think this happened? _____

_____

_____

NOTE: If you have a vegetable garden separate from the habitat garden your group is creating, you may be struggling between wanting to have wildlife in a habitat area and wanting to protect your group's vegetable and fruit plants until harvest time. This activity will help your students have the best of both worlds. As a part of their wildlife gardening effort, your group is working to attract wildlife. By using a little creativity and some recycled items, the students can work to establish their tomatoes, corn, or any other specific plants as less appealing to wildlife.

Any materials can be used for this activity. You may want to ask the JMGers beforehand to bring milk jugs, soda bottles, foil, unwanted CDs, etc. Reusing materials that would typically be thrown away is a great way to recycle.

Ask the gardeners if they know the purpose of using a scarecrow. Tell them that farmers and gardeners have used scarecrows for thousands of years to keep certain birds away that might cause damage to food crops. The scarecrow does this without harming the bird. It was believed that if a scarecrow looked like a person standing in a field, the hungry crow would stay away. Other safe methods such as creating movement, flashes of light or reflections that startle have been used to keep certain birds

other animals away from a crop. Many other objects can be used to distance birds from a certain garden.

If your wildlife garden area is attracting animals to your group's tempting fruits and vegetables growing in another area, challenge your group to find a safe way to deter wildlife from visiting those specific plants. Students might decorate a stake that can be placed near the plant and topped with long ribbons that will cause movement when the wind blows or they

might recycle used CDs to create a mobile that reflects light and movement.

Divide class into groups of 2-3. Tell the gardeners that they are going to design deterrents for birds using the materials that have been collected. Have them create a list of the materials they would like to work with and sketch a design. Groups should plan a time to gather and bring materials in with them to begin building their deterrents.

After everyone has finished, have a "show and tell" for all of the deterrents that the group can set in the garden and put to the test. At the very least these modern "scarecrows" will serve as temporary and interesting garden art!

In the Classroom

If your group has already experienced some damage to fruits and vegetables, have them survey the damage each day over a week before placing the deterrent near the plants. Have students determine the following:

- What specific plants are being damaged?

- How many plants are being damaged?

- How often does the damage occur?

- How much damage is taking place each day/night?

By observing and collecting specific data about the damage before the deterrents are placed near a plant, students can establish how effective the deterrent has been.

Wildlife:
Mammals

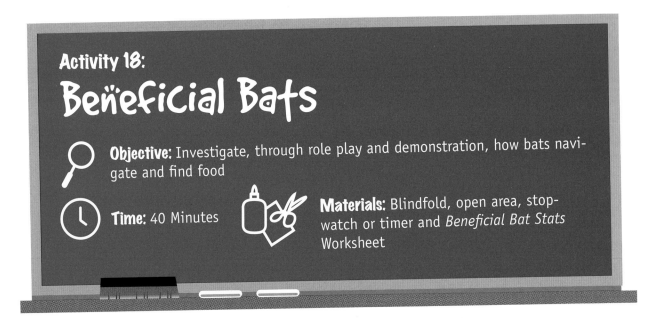

Activity 18:
Beneficial Bats

Objective: Investigate, through role play and demonstration, how bats navigate and find food

Time: 40 Minutes

Materials: Blindfold, open area, stopwatch or timer and *Beneficial Bat Stats* Worksheet

Ask the group to draw a picture of a bat. Give them a few minutes to complete their drawings. As they work, ask them to talk about what a bat is. Have them to describe what a bat looks like, how a bat acts and what a bat eats. As you discuss bats with your group you likely will find a great deal of misinformation about these small creatures. Share the bat facts with your students and stress that bats can be very beneficial to a garden setting because they consume a great number of insects.

Ask your Wildlife Gardeners if they have ever heard the expression "as blind as a bat". Explain that although bats are not really blind, and some do have poor eyesight, poor vision does not cause problems for bats. Bats have adapted to find food a very different way and have developed another way of "seeing" what is around them. They use **echolocation** to sense what is around them and to find food. Bats squeak as they fly. Their squeaks bounce off objects and they hear

the echoes. This allows them to sense the location of an object so they do not fly into it. This also allows them to find food, such as mosquitoes and other insects that fill the night sky.

Tell the group that they are going to play the *Echolocation Game*. Divide the class into two groups. Select one person from each group to be a bat. Have the first group spread out to form a large circle with the second group inside. Tie a bandanna or cloth around the "bat's"

head to make a blindfold. The students inside the circle will be pesky insects–mosquitoes in this game. The mosquitoes should fold their arms and "fly" about the circle. The first group that forms the circle contains the mosquitoes and keeps the blindfolded bat from wandering away from the group.

The bat walks around the area and squeaks. The mosquitoes must immitate or make an echo of the bat's squeak. The bat can track each mosquito by its echo. To "eat" the mosquito, the bat touches the person echoing the squeak. The "eaten" mosquito should step outside the circle. Allow the bat to "feed" for no more than one minute. After time is up, determine how many insects the bat ate. If possible, allow each gardener the chance to be a bat for one minute.

Be sure to discuss safety before beginning the *Echolocation Game*. No running is allowed and students should be careful not to bump into the hungry bat when the bat is blindfolded.

When the game is over, ask how many insects the bats ate. Pass out the *Beneficial Bat Stats worksheet* to each student. Ask the group to guess how many insects a single bat can consume in one hour and record their guesses. Tell the group that bats can eat as many as 1000 insects in one hour. Have the group determine the following:

- How many insects are eaten if one bat feeds for two hours?

- How many insects are eaten if three bats feed for one hour?

Bat Facts

- Bats are mammals.

- Bats are the only mammals capable of true flight.

- Bats consume many insects considered pests.

- Bats that eat fruit and drink nectar help disperse seed and are important pollinators.

- Bats are very clean and spend a great of their resting times grooming themselves.

- Bats rest, hibernate and even bear young hanging upside down.

- Bats can find very unconventional living spaces by roosting from the roof of a caves, hollow trees or foliage, barn ceilings, attic and even under bridges.

- Bats can be found on every continent except Antarctica.

- How many insects are eaten if 10 bats feed for five hours?

Tell the group that bat colonies often consist of thousands of bats. Together, determine how many insects 2000 bats could eat in a two-hour period. In five hours?

Have the students create a graph showing the number of insects a single bat can consume if feeding for five hours a night. The graph should track the cumulative daily total of insects consumed daily for a month. Have students use the graph to estimate the number of insects consumed over a 10-year life span.

Finally, have each Wildlife Gardener create a poster to be used as a public service announcement to educate others about beneficial bats.

For more information about bats, including how to create a bat house to add to your garden habitat area, visit the resource links at *www.jmgkids.org/wildlifegardener*

In the Classroom

Ask the group *how* they hear sounds. Explain that sound travels in waves and we can hear it once sound waves hit our ears. The same is true for bats. Ask the group to describe a wave. What makes waves? They probably associate waves with water. Reiterate that sound travels in waves too. We can't see sound waves, but they are present.

Have everyone stand up side by side. Tell the group that they are going to pretend to be a wave. You are going to start the wave by touching a person on one end of the line. That person will raise his/her hands and then put them back down. The next person should do the same. Everyone follows until the last person finishes.

Cut a piece of plastic wrap that is large enough to cover a cake pan with overlap (a 9"x12" pans works well). Place the wrap on top of the cake pan and stretch it so that there are no wrinkles. Secure it tightly with tape. Scatter brown sugar or flour on the plastic. Hold the cookie sheet above the cake pan. Hit the cookie sheet with the spoon. The flour will bounce.

Explain to the group that the flour bounced because sound waves traveled from the cookie sheet to the cake pan and vibrated the plastic. Just as the sound waves caused the movement in the plastic, sound waves travel to our ears and cause movement in our ear drums, allowing us to hear.

Beneficial Bat Stats

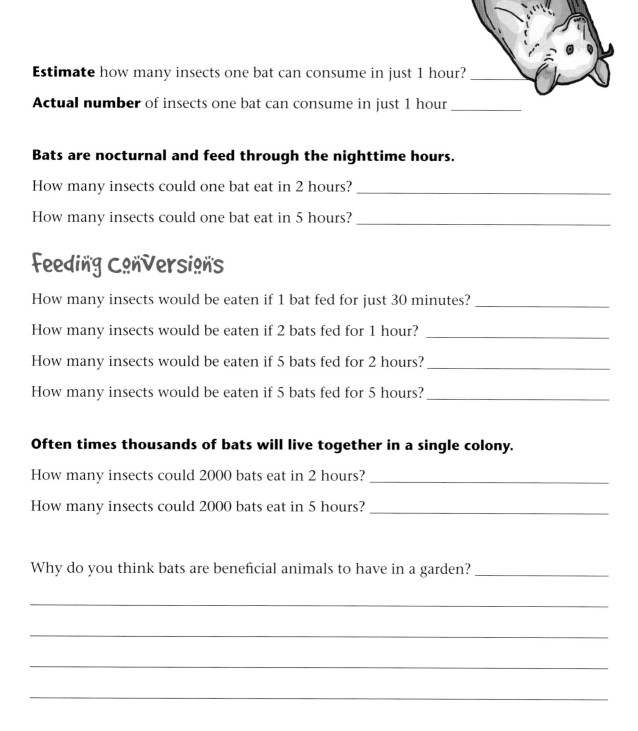

Estimate how many insects one bat can consume in just 1 hour? _____

Actual number of insects one bat can consume in just 1 hour _____

Bats are nocturnal and feed through the nighttime hours.

How many insects could one bat eat in 2 hours? _____

How many insects could one bat eat in 5 hours? _____

Feeding Conversions

How many insects would be eaten if 1 bat fed for just 30 minutes? _____

How many insects would be eaten if 2 bats fed for 1 hour? _____

How many insects would be eaten if 5 bats fed for 2 hours? _____

How many insects would be eaten if 5 bats fed for 5 hours? _____

Often times thousands of bats will live together in a single colony.

How many insects could 2000 bats eat in 2 hours? _____

How many insects could 2000 bats eat in 5 hours? _____

Why do you think bats are beneficial animals to have in a garden? _____

_____

_____

_____

_____

Activity 19:
Master Mammal Minds

Objective: Develop an understanding of animals through research and creative writing

Time: 40 Minutes

Materials: *Master Mammal Minds* page, pencil and paper

Have the Wildlife Gardeners try to guess the mystery mammal described below:

- I'm a mammal and am more clever than you probably know.

- If you see me it's probably at night.

- Some people think I'm mischievous and I wear a mask!

Give them a few guesses before providing the answer: I'm a raccoon.

Share the mammal facts with the group. Ask the group if people belong in this category. Point out that humans belong in the same class as squirrels, mountain lions and even raccoons.

Divide the class into two groups. Give each group two minutes to brainstorm a list of as many mammals as they can. When time is up, have each side take turns adding one of the mammals on their list as you write them on a chalkboard or poster. As each animal is suggested, have the group confirm that it is a mammal before listing it. Have students add a star to any animals that the group thinks might be found in your area and that could possibly visit your garden area.

Mammal Facts

- Mammals have fur or hair.

- Mammals produce milk for their young.

- Mammals are warm blooded.

- Almost all mammals give birth to live young.

- Mammals sweat (like people) or pant (like dogs) to cool themselves.

- Mammals live in many different habitats all over the world.

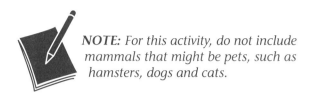
NOTE: *For this activity, do not include mammals that might be pets, such as hamsters, dogs and cats.*

Allow students to work as partners and select one of the starred animals to learn about and become a Master Mammal Mind–an expert about their mammal. Pass out a *Master Mammal Minds* Facts page to each student. Allow students access to reference materials and online resources available through *www.jmgkids.org/wildlifegardener* to complete the facts about their mammal.

Once students have each completed their *Master Mammal Minds* page, allow each group one minute to share with the rest of the group some of the interesting facts about their local mammals that they learned.

4

Master Mammal Minds

Mammal: _____

This animal is ☐ nocturnal *(active at night)*

☐ diurnal *(active during the day)*

This animal is ☐ a carnivore *(eats only meat)*

☐ herbivore *(eats only plants)*

☐ omnivore *(eats plants & meat)*

sketch the paw print of your mammal here:

This animal might be seen living in (describe its habitat – such as woodlands, desert, rocky areas, riverbanks, prairies, farmlands, or others): _____

_____

Color in the areas of the map below that this animal lives:

Description of mammal: _____

_____

color of fur: _____

long fur or short fur: _____

tail or no tail: _____

☐ **special markings** ☐ **no special markings**

Other cool facts about this animal: _____

_____

_____

On the back:
If your animal is an herbivore or an omnivore, write at least one plant that it eats.

72

Activity 20:
Two Sides to Every Story

Objective: Explore a situation from differing points of view

Time: 40 Minutes

Materials: Paper, pencils, crayons or markers

Ask for two volunteers. Make sure the two volunteers have recently been involved in the same activity, such as taking a spelling test or completing a JMG activity. Ask one of the volunteers to step outside of the room or to cover his ears so that he cannot hear what is being said. Have the other person to recall his experience to the rest of the group and include as many details as possible. Then ask the first person to do the same. Note any differences in the two accounts for the group. Explain to the group that two people can experience the same occurrence, but each person can view it in a different way.

Tell the group that just like people, wildlife need and use plants in our gardens. For example, a bird may like to eat tomatoes from a vegetable garden. But, just like the situation above, there are two sides to the story. A gardener may become angry at the bird because his/her tomatoes have been eaten. But, to the bird, the tomatoes are food. The bird does not know that the tomatoes may be "off limits" because the gardener wants to eat them.

Tell the JMGers that you are going to tell them a story from a gardener's point of view. Afterwards, each person will write the same story told from the animal's point of view.

The Gardener's Side of the Story:

My name is Kelly and I like to grow fruits and vegetables in my garden. But, lately a pesky squirrel has been making me mad. I have a peach tree in my backyard. Every year my tree produces tasty, sweet peaches. This year, I didn't have many peaches to eat. My tree produced fruit, but that squirrel ate the peaches before I could! He climbed into the tree and grabbed a peach. Then I saw him take a few bites and throw the peach on the ground. Then, he grabbed another peach. He took a few bites and then threw that one to the ground too. He didn't even eat the whole thing! How greedy!

I had some herbs growing in a pretty container. But, that same squirrel ruined them. He dug a hole in the container and planted some nuts in it. When he dug the hole, he hurt the roots of some of the herb plants. Most of them died. That squirrel is driving my crazy!

I don't know about you, but I like to feed birds. So, I made a bird feeder and hung it in a tree in my yard. I filled it with seeds.

That little squirrel thought the feeder was for him. He climbed into the tree, jumped onto the feeder, and started eating the seeds. He ate and ate. He ate so much that there weren't any seeds for the birds to eat! Oh! I'm starting to really dislike that squirrel!

Now ask each gardener to write about this same event but to write it from the squirrel's point of view. Afterwards, ask each person to read her story to the rest of the group.

74

In the Classroom

Critter Court

Discuss with the group the fact that sometimes people cannot compromise with one another and have to find someone else to help them reach an agreement. People sometimes go to court to help settle arguments. A judge is a person who works in a court and makes judgments to ensure that laws are being followed. People often hire lawyers to help them explain their side of the story.

Tell the group that they are going to hold a mock trial for the gardener and squirrel they read about in the "Two Sides to Every Story" activity. The gardener and squirrel should each explain their sides of the story to their respective lawyers. The gardener's lawyer should cross-examine the squirrel and the squirrel's lawyer should cross-examine the gardener. The judge is to keep order in the court. If someone becomes too loud and disorderly, the judge is the person who should restore order to the group. The jury members should listen carefully to both sides of the story as they are presented in court. After the trial, ask the jury to vote on whether they think the squirrel is guilty of doing something wrong. (If there are no more than five people in the group, have the judge decide the outcome.) Then ask the entire group to think of a compromise for the gardener and squirrel so that they can coexist peacefully.

Ask for volunteers to play the following roles:

Gardener	Squirrel
Gardener's Lawyer	Squirrel's Lawyer
Judge	Jury Members (if the group is larger than 5)

Activity 21:
Critter Critique

🔍 **Objective:** Investigate other people's opinions and experiences with wildlife

🕐 **Time:** 45-60 Minutes

✂️ **Materials:** *Critter Critique* pages (3 per person), chalk board and chalk or poster board and markers

NOTE: *At least one day prior to this activity assign each JMGer to use the* Critter Critique *pages and poll three adults about wildlife. The poll focuses on people's understanding of wildlife; specifically, what types of mammals people like and dislike, and what experiences people have had with any type of wildlife.*

After the polling is done, record the following information on the chalkboard or poster board:

1. How many people like to attract and/or watch wildlife?

2. What types of mammals did people most want to see?

3. What types of mammals did people least want to see?

4. What did people like about wildlife?

5. How many people had experiences some type of damage caused by wildlife?

6. What are some things that people did to stop the damage?

7. Which of the following items did people mark as true?

A. If you want wildlife in your yard/garden, you have to tolerate some damage.

　☐ True　☐ False

B. Most forms of wildlife are very beneficial to a yard/garden.

　☐ True　☐ False

C. Examples of mammals are squirrels, raccoons, bats and rabbits.

　☐ True　☐ False

D. Wildlife that visit my yard/garden are looking for food, water or shelter.

　☐ True　☐ False

Discuss the results with the group. If possible, have student help to create a

group bar graph showing the results to questions 2, 3 and 5.

Look at the list for questions 2 and 3. Discuss with the group why people might like certain types of wildlife but not others. For example, if someone said that they would most like to see a rabbit in their yard, ask the group to think of why this may be. If someone said that they would least like to see a mouse in their backyard, ask the group to think of their opinions of why people stated that.

Ask the group if they have the same feelings as those seen in the poll. Have

the students complete a *Critter Critique* page themselves. Using a different colored chalk or marker, record the group's responses to the same questions. Tell the group that when people learn more about something, they will better understand it. And when people are more knowledgeable about something, they can make a well informed decision. As Junior Master Gardeners learning about wildlife, it is their responsibility to share what they learn with others.

In the Classroom

Have the class follow up with a second poll that focus on people's least favorite and most favorite mammals and why people have those opinions. First, have students create a list of several mammals that are likely to live in your community. The group can begin by brainstorming a list of the mammals they believe are or might be local and then research through reference materials or resource links available at _www.jmgkids.org/wildlifegardener_ to confirm that those mammals are in your region.

Next, have students poll at least three adults by asking them to vote for their least favorite and most favorite mammal from the list. Have students ask why they consider those animals their least and most favorite.

On a chalkboard or poster board, make a list of the local mammals from the poll. Beside each mammal, have students create two rows of tallies: red tally marks for votes that mammal received for being a least favorite and blue tally marks for being voted a most favorite. Have students convert the data into a bar graph showing the results.

Then have the students share some of their reasons people gave for voting the way they did. Write on the chalkboard/poster each different answer the students share. When all of the responses are recorded, have the group help you determine if each of the statements are a fact or opinion by writing an "F" or "O" beside each.

Have the students use the information they learned from the polling to determine which mammals they want to attract to their garden habitat area.

critter critique

1. Do you like to attract and/or watch wildlife in your backyard? _____

2. What type of **mammal** would you MOST like to see visit your backyard? _____
_____

3. What type of **mammal** would you LEAST like to see visit your backyard? _____
_____

4. What do you like about wildlife visiting your backyard? _____
_____
_____

4

5. Have any animals caused damage to your garden or other parts of your yard? _____

6. What type of animal and what type of damage? _____
_____
_____

7. What did you do to stop it (if anything)? _____

8. Which items below do you think are true?

☐ A. If you want wildlife in your yard/garden, you have to tolerate some damage.

☐ B. Most forms of wildlife are very beneficial to a yard/garden .

☐ C. Examples of mammals are squirrels, raccoons. bats and rabbits.

☐ D. Wildlife that visits my yard/garden are looking for food, water or shelter.

Wildlife:
Insects

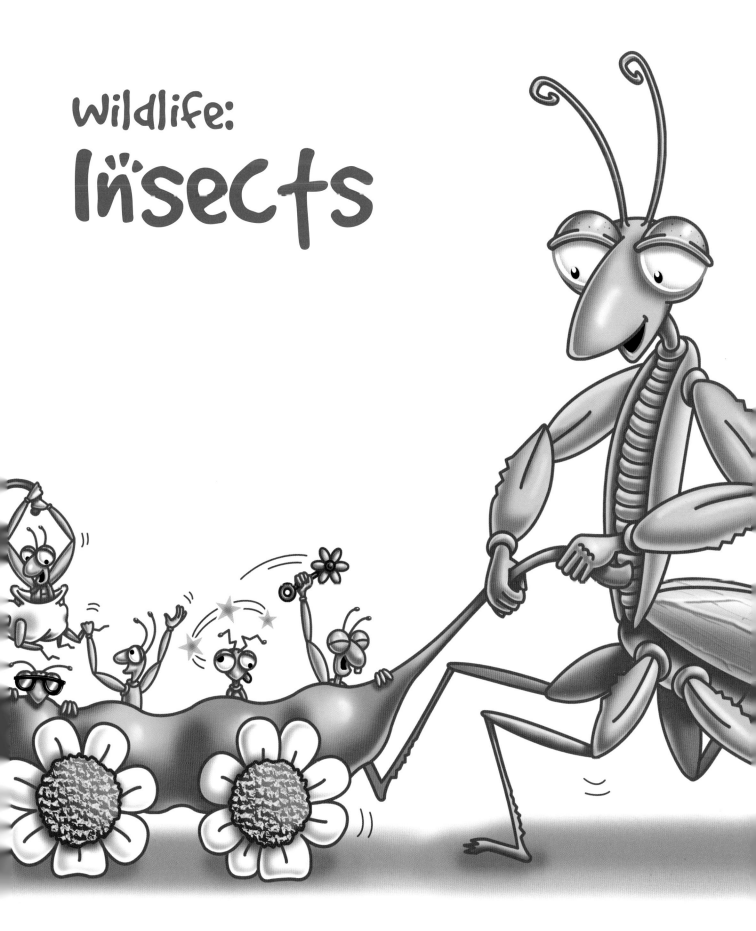

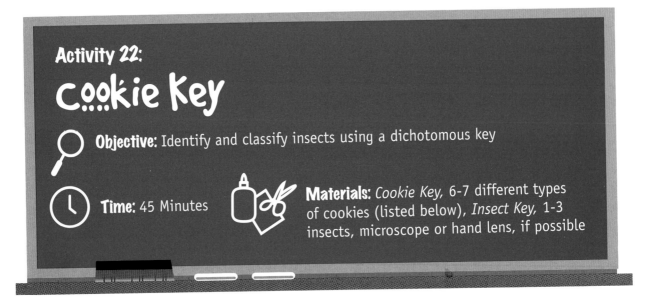

Activity 22:
cookie key

Objective: Identify and classify insects using a dichotomous key

Time: 45 Minutes

Materials: *Cookie Key*, 6-7 different types of cookies (listed below), *Insect Key*, 1-3 insects, microscope or hand lens, if possible

NOTE: Prior to this activity be adventurous and try to capture several insects for the group to identify. Insects that are easier to "key out" are listed on pages 83 and 87. Baby food jars with air holes make great observation chambers!

Ask the group what they would do if they saw an odd looking insect and wanted to know what type of insect it was. The majority of the group will probably say "Ask someone." Tell the group that they can find out on their own by using an insect key. Explain that a key is a tool that people can use to help them find out the names of animals and plants based on the characteristics of how they look. Tell the group that to learn how to use a key, they are first going to use a Cookie Key!

Divide the JMGers into groups of 2-3. Give each group a copy of the Cookie Key on the next page and 1 of each of the following types of cookies:

• Animal cookie

• Butter cookie

• Chocolate chip cookie

• Chocolate sandwich cookie

• Fig bar

• Ginger snap

• Lemon cookie

Tell the groups that a key has two sentences labeled "1," two sentences labeled "2," and so on. The two sentences in each set have contrasting information describing what you are trying to identify. At the end of each sentence, there is either another choice or the answer.

To give the group the experience of working with a key, tell them that they are going to use a Cookie Key. Explain that you want them to pretend that they do not know what any of the cookies are and that they'll be using them to practice keying. The Cookie Key flow chart on page 84 may help students visualize how the key works.

Cookie Key

1. This cookie is soft . . . . **fig bar**

1. This cookie is hard . . . . **Go to 2**

2. This cookie has chocolate in or on it . . . . **Go to 3**

2. This cookie does not have chocolate in or on it . . . . **Go to 4**

3. This cookie has chocolate pieces . . . . **chocolate chip cookie**

3. This cookie has filling . . . . **chocolate sandwich cookie**

4. This cookie is shaped like an animal . . . . **animal cookie**

4. This cookie is not shaped like an animal . . . . **Go to 5**

5. This cookie has a hole in the middle . . . . **Go to 6**

5. This cookie does not have a hole in the middle . . . . **ginger snap**

6. This cookie tastes like lemon . . . . **lemon cookie**

6. This cookie tastes like butter . . . . **butter cookie**

Allow the groups to share and eat the cookies when they are finished!

Tell the youths that insects can be identified using a key, too. Pass out an insect to each group and challenge them to use the insect key to identify it.

Have them use the Insect Key, page 86, to determine what Order (a type of group) the insect(s) belongs to. This key can come in handy when trying to tell the good guys from the bad guys in your garden habitat area.

Have the students take home a copy of their Insect Key to show a family member how to use a key to identify an insect that they find around their home.

The following are easy to "key out":

Ladybugs	Ants
Grasshoppers	Butterflies
Crickets	Flies
Aphids	Stink bugs

Cookie Key Flow Chart

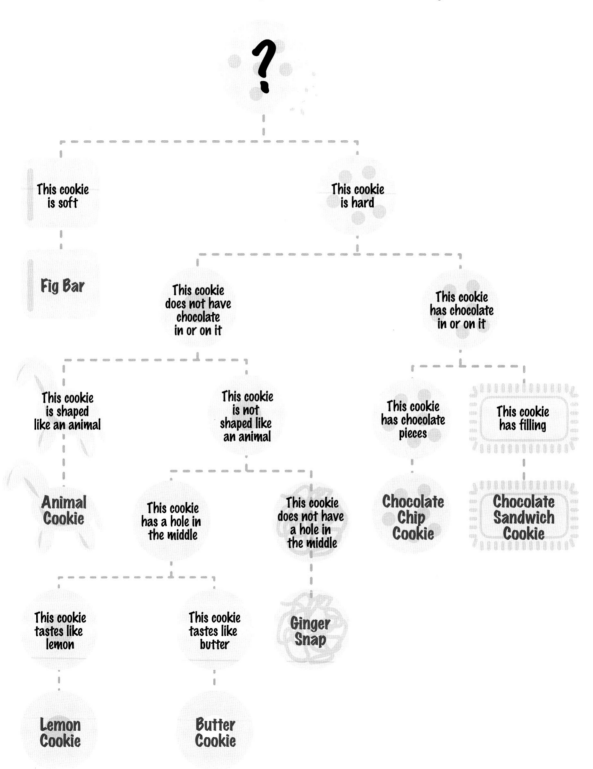

In the Classroom

Have students use magnifying glasses to examine the insects collected paying close attention to the mouth parts. After the group has identified the insect type of mouthpart, have them make a sketch of it. Ask the group to think about their own mouths. Which insect mouth part is most like their own? Explain that over time different insects have inherited more and more specialized mouthparts help them be more successful at consuming a certain type of food available in their environment.

Point out that insects with those mouthparts are a part of the system within the habitat. For example, some insects, such as grasshoppers, can cause damage to plants with their chewing mouthparts, but may also be the primary food source for a host of other wildlife during certain times of the year. And not only are butterflies beautiful bouncing from flower to flower with their siphoning mouthparts, they are also feeding on nectar and serving the vital role of pollinating the flowers they are visiting.

5

Insect Key

1. Insect has six legs . . . . **Go to 2**

1. It has less than or more than six legs . . . . **Not an insect**

2. Insect has one pair of wings (two wings total) . . . . **Order Diptera**

2. Insect has two pairs of wings (four wings total) . . . . **Go to 3**

3. Mouthparts are sucking or piercing/sucking type (see below) . . . . **Go to 4**

3. Mouthparts are chewing (see below) . . . . **Go to 6**

4. Body is thin and narrow . . . . **Order Lepidoptera**

4. Body is wide . . . . **Go to 5**

5. Wings overlap to form a triangle shape . . . . **Order Hemiptera**

5. Wings form a "tent" over the body or it has no wings . . . . **Order Homoptera**

6. It has a thin and narrow "waist" . . . . **Order Hymenoptera**

6. It's "waist" is not narrow . . . . **Go to 7**

7. Wings form a straight line down the back when folded
   and all legs are about the same size (see below) . . . . **Order Coleoptera**

7. Wings do not form a straight line down the
   back when folded and some legs is larger than the
   others (see below) . . . . **Order Orthoptera**

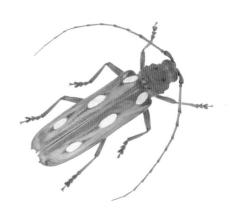

Mouthparts

Wings

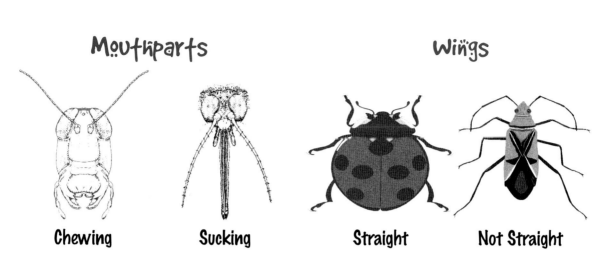

Chewing   Sucking   Straight   Not Straight

Did you know?

Order Coleoptera
includes lady bugs, June bugs, and other beetles

Order Diptera
includes flies, mosquitoes, and gnats

Order Hemiptera
includes stink bugs and beetles

Order Homoptera
includes aphids, scale, and cicadas

Order Hymenoptera
includes ants, bees, and wasps

Order Lepidoptera
includes butterflies and moths

Order Orthoptera
includes cockroaches, crickets, and grasshoppers

5

Activity 23:
The Great Cover Up

Objective: Experience the effectiveness of how insect use camouflage

Time: 30 Minutes

Materials: Insect Templates pages (in appendix), paper and crayons and/or markers

Before the activity, copy and cut the insect templates and color them using those colors and/or patterns around you. For example, color in one of the insects similar to the color of a chalkboard, another to have a wood-grain look similar to a desk top or coat rack, another that is the color of a countertop, etc. Before the students come in, tape the insects to the various surfaces that they match.

This activity can be adapted for outdoors using natural materials (leaves, grass, soil) as the insect templates are being camouflaged.

To introduce the following discussion, you might want to wear army fatigue-type clothes such as camouflage pants or t-shirt, if available, to stimulate gardeners' interest.

Lead students in a conversation about the concept of camouflage. Ask them what they think camouflage is. They may have heard the term before in reference to camouflage clothing worn by members of the military. Ask students what camouflage clothing looks like. What is its purpose? Through discussion, make sure that students know that the purpose of camouflage clothing is to conceal the person wearing it. Camouflage is a type of disguise that hides people (or animals) by helping them blend in with their surroundings. In addition to people in the military, many animals and plants use camouflage either to allow them to sneak up on their prey, or to hide from a predator.

Tell students that, before they came in, you placed some insect shapes around the room. Let them know how many there are. Ask them to pretend that they are hungry predators looking for a juicy insect snack. Keep track of the time it takes for them to find all of the insects. Afterwards, discuss camouflage again. Were the insects well hidden?

How long did it take to find all of the shapes? If the insects had been real and the students real predators, which ones would have been caught and eaten first? What advantage is there in being well camouflaged? Explain that insects have adapted over time to be able to hide and protect themselves from predators and to to conceal themselves from their prey.

Some insects use **reverse-camouflage**. That is, they are brightly colored so they stand out rather than hide. Usually, these insects taste bad or are toxic, and the bright colors serve as a **"DO NOT EAT!"** warning to other animals. Other insects use bright colors to disguise themselves as a toxic or bad-tasting insect. This technique of imitation is called **mimicry**. Pretty tricky, huh?

Take the group for a nature walk and challenge them to find four examples of camouflaged insects. Remind them of safety rules and to not actually touch the insects but instead point it out to others. There are likely many insects students will look past, as they are doing a very good job of hiding in plain sight. For photos of some of the most effectively camouflaged insects, visit the links at: www.jmgkids.org/wildlifegardener

5

Activity 24:
Backyard Butterflies

Objective: Create a butterfly garden

Time: Variable

Materials: For the planning stage: 1 sheet of grid/graph paper per group (in appendix), paper, transparency of grid, overhead projector, transparency markers, crayons or colored pencils, clipboards, scissors, pencils, glue or tape. For implementing the garden: plants, shovels, water supply, flat rock, and a shallow container

 NOTE: When planning and implementing any new gardening project, refer to the Garden Preparation and Planting Instructions in the appendix.

Ask the gardeners if they would like to have butterflies in their garden. Ask the group how they think butterflies are beneficial to a garden. Remind them that butterflies aid in the pollination of many plants. Point out there are other more intangible benefits as well, such as adding color and movement to a garden area. Many people find watching butterflies relaxing; they are beneficial for people as well.

Choose a site for a butterfly garden. If time allows, get your JMGers involved in the selection process and use P.L.A.N.T. and Wildlife Needs (Activity #1, page 2) to help choose the spot. The following guidelines for butterfly gardening should help when you are looking for a site for your butterfly garden:

1. Look for windbreaks. Butterflies are delicate and need protection from gusty winds. Tall plant material, such as trees and shrubs, and other windbreaks, such as berms, walls, fences and buildings or other structures can provide shelter from windy conditions. Point out the direction of the prevailing winds in your area so the existing windbreaks are offering protection to your selected area.

2. Provide a sunny area for basking. Butterflies like to sun themselves, so be sure that your site has a patch of sun. Placing a flat rock in the sun is a great idea.

3. Butterflies need shallow water. Place a shallow dish/container in your garden to provide a source of water for butterflies.

4. Add plants that are attractive to butterflies. A plant list follows, but check with your county Extension office or contact a local nursery to find out which plants are recommended specifically for your area.

Plant lists

For larva:

Parsley	Sunflower	Dill	Willow	Nettle
Hibiscus	Milkweed	Passionflower	Violet	
Hollyhock	Wild Senna	Salvia	Elm	

For adult butterflies:

Buttonbush	Lantana	Passionflower	Verbena
Hibiscus	Milkweed	Salvia	Zinnia
Hollyhock	Marigold	Sunflower	

NOTE: Once the list of potential plants has been decided, investigate the mature size of each one and create a symbol to scale for each plant. The scale can be set to 1 square foot = 1 square inch as is the grid paper in the appendix. Each group will be using these to design the butterfly garden. Draw several copies of the symbol on a page and copy the page. These butterfly plant symbols will be needed for each landscaping team described below!

Have the students help measure the dimensions of the site you have selected, allowing one block on the grid for one square foot of garden space. Back inside, show the group how to draw those dimensions onto a grid on the overhead projector. Point out the length of each side and have the students determine the perimeter (total length of the sides) of the space as well as the area (total number of squares contained within the lines) in square feet. Divide the JMGers into smaller groups of 2-3 and have them recreate the outlines of the dimensions of the space on their own grid paper.

Each small group will be a landscaping team. Take the group back outside and have them take additional measurements to record the location and the area that any existing trees, shrubs, and buildings or other structures occupy. Ask each group to draw these objects on their graph paper. Be sure to tell your landscapers the direction of the prevailing winds in your area so windbreaks are placed in the appropriate areas.

On another sheet of paper, each group should create symbols and a map key to represent windbreaks, plant material, water sources and rocks. They can cut out the symbols and begin arranging them on their pages. Then ask each group to begin planning the butterfly garden by arranging the butterfly plant symbols on their landscape plans. If your JMGers want to add anything else to their garden, such as statuary, sundials, etc., have each group draw a symbol for that as well.

Afterwards, have everyone view all of the landscape plans and discuss them. Vote on which plan will be carried out. If the group cannot reach consensus, consider combining ideas from several plans to make the final plan. When the plan is set, it is time to acquire the seeds or transplants.

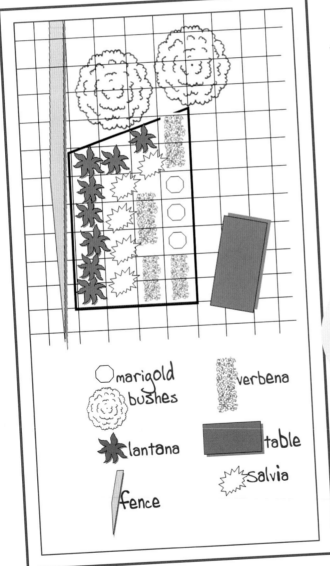

marigold
bushes

verbena

lantana

table

salvia

fence

Remember to review safety rules when working in the garden.

Once your group has discussed how the Backyard Butterfly Garden will be maintained (see Schedule It, Activity 5, page 12), they can get to work! Plan a garden work day (page 187) with parents or other adults if extra help is needed such as helping bring in large amounts of soil, move heavier plants, etc. Either way, let your JMGers get their hands dirty during planting. They'll love it and develop a sense of pride and ownership from being part of the effort. Be sure to follow planting instructions on plant and seed labels. Soon a beautiful butterfly garden will slowly emerge from even the most unsightly locations.

In the Classroom

Studying butterflies provides a natural context for strengthening students' understanding of symmetry. Have students research reference materials or online links at *www.jmgkids.org/wildlifegardener* by finding their favorite butterfly. Students may choose a butterfly because of its beautiful markings, because it is local to the area, or because they've seen one in real life. Find an image that shows the wing spread of their butterfly. Have them recreate that shape and pattern on a sheet of construction paper. Encourage them to do so in perfect symmetry, just like the real butterflies!

First have them fold the paper in half and draw a line in the middle to create the line of symmetry. On one side of the paper, have them use a pencil to make a sketch of the wing that includes the outline of the edge of the wing and the markings inside the shape. Next, they should use paint brushes and carefully paint and recreate individual markings that make up that butterfly's distinctive pattern. After each individual marking is painted, have the students fold the paper over and press it to produce the perfect symmetrical image on the opposite side. Have them continue until the entire wing is carefully. painted and reproduced on the opposite side. Butterflies should them be cut, labeled on the back with the type of butterfly it is and hung from the ceiling.

5

Activity 25:

Metamorphosis Song

Objective: Demonstrate understanding of the life cycles of the butterfly

Time: 45 Minutes

Materials: Copies of the *Metamorphosis Song*, page 97, crayons or markers, scissors, hole punch, scissors and yarn or string

Insects go through different life stages as they grow. This process is called metamorphosis, which means "change of form." Some insects, such as butterflies, change form completely as they go through the different stages. Their larval form, caterpillars, look very different and even have different types of mouthparts from their adult form as butterflies. Other types of insects may look similar to their adult forms throughout their life.

There are two different types of metamorphosis: *complete* and *incomplete*. The insects grouped together in an order all go through the same type of metamorphosis. The stages of each type of metamorphosis are pictured on the next page.

Ask the students to cut out pictures of each stage of the life cycle in complete metamorphosis (egg, larva, pupa, and adult) from the *Metamorphosis Song*, page 97. Have students use a hole punch

to make a hole at each end of the cut out shape, and tie a piece of string through the holes. Tie all four pictures together, making a chain that can be used as a metamorphosis bracelet or belt. They can add colorful beads or other decorations between the four segments, if they wish. Continue to ask questions and discuss these stages of metamorphosis as the students work. When everyone is done, emphasize the ongoing cyclical aspect of life cycles.

To conclude, have the students divide into three groups and give them 10 minutes to practice before performing the *Metamorphosis Song* to review what they leaned about complete metamorphosis. There is no specific tune to the Metamorphosis Song. Students can be creative and perform as a rap, a dramatic poetry reading, or any other form they want.

complete Metamorphosis: egg, larva, pupa, adult

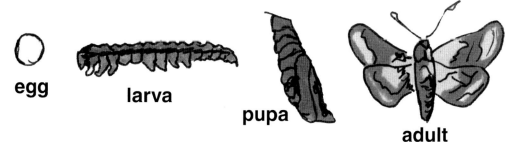

egg   larva   pupa   adult

An adult insect lays its **eggs** in a protected place where hatching larvae will be able to find food easily. When larvae hatch, they are eating machines! As they grow, they shed their skin several times. Their skeleton is on the outside of their bodies, so it cannot expand and grow with them. When they have reached full size as **larvae**, they are ready for the next stage, called the **pupa** (plural: pupae). The larvae may form a cocoon(for moths), or chrysalis(for butterflies). Inside the cocoon the insect's body changes form, and is transformed into the **adult** form. Then the adult insect breaks out of the cocoon, mates, and the cycle starts over again.

Incomplete Metamorphosis: egg, nymph, adult

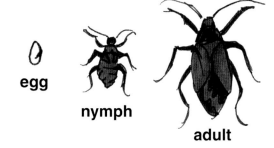

egg   nymph   adult

There are several types of incomplete metamorphosis. Insects that go through incomplete metamorphosis may change features somewhat as they grow, may change very little except for the addition of such features as wings, or may not change at all. Some insects with this type of metamorphosis may live part of their lives underwater as aquatic insects. During incomplete metamorphosis, insects still go through growth stages where they shed their skin; however, they don't completely change their form (such as caterpillar to butterfly), as insects do in complete metamorphosis.

In the Classroom

Have students create a list of stages of the human life cycle. Have them write one sentence that describes what happens at each stage. Challenge them to draw a connection to which of the stages of the human life cycle most closely match with a stage in the butterflies life cycle.

Have the students research to find examples of life cycles of different organisms such as plants, frogs and other animals. Then challenge the group create a life cycle collage that includes images and labels for life cycles and stages of all other researched organisms. Once the collage is complete, have the student describe their contributions to the cycle collage.

The Metamorphosis Song

Group one:

A butterfly flew,
Around the sky one day.
She saw the perfect plant,
Safe place to lay her eggs
Laid in a secret place
On a leaf's underside
First stage of this life cycle
The eggs could grow and hide.

Chorus:

From an egg into larva
Pupa, adult makes the list
Stages of life cycle called

COMPLETE METAMORPH-O-SIS!

Group Two:

Time passed and passed
The eggs seemed still and stiller.
Suddenly out from an egg
Crawled a hungry caterpillar.

This stage of life.
Larva - a butterfly child,
It's small but very hungry
Eats through leaves like wild!

Group Three:

Big caterpillar said proudly,
My life cycle keeps going
There's one more thing I have to do-
So I can keep on growing.
Big changes would soon happen,
During metamorphosis,
Built a room for itself,
Called a chrysalis.
(kriss-uh-liss)

All:

After a few more weeks
Amazing change took place inside
An egg, larva then a pupa
Now's a winged adult butterfly.

5

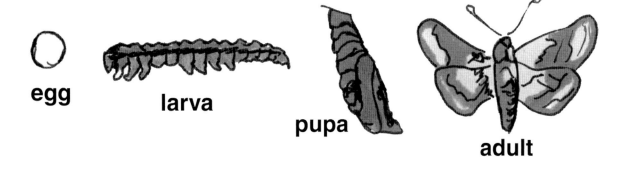

egg   **larva**   **pupa**   **adult**

97

Activity 26:
Who Goes There?

🔍 **Objective:** Learn the basics of Integrated Pest Management (IPM), and create a classroom IPM charting system

🕐 **Time:** 1 hour plus 15 minutes for pest check two times per week

✂️ **Materials:** Paper and pencils

Managing the garden is very important and will make a big difference in how well the group's garden grows. Gardeners and professional horticulturists use a style of managing pests called IPM, which stands for Integrated Pest Management. IPM is a method of managing pests in a way that is environmentally friendly. The steps involved in IPM are discussed in the What is IPM? section on page 100.

A simplified version of IPM can be used with your JMGers by using the chart on the next page. Assist your group in following the steps of the flow chart to resolve pest outbreaks in your garden.

Ask students to scout in the garden each week to see what types of insects or signs of insect damage they see. For each insect, go through the flow chart process to determine what action needs to be taken. This can be done as an activity for several weeks, but is best used on an ongoing basis as a regular garden maintenance duty.

Integrated Pest Management Chart

(Draw me here)

Am I Beneficial?
Leave me alone and let me work for you.

Am I a Pest?

Are there just a few of us on your plant?
Pick us off with your hands and squash us!

Are there lots of us on your plant?
Spray with water to knock us off your plant.

Did this work?

Yes
Congratulations, you did it!

No
Can the plant be removed?

Yes
Remove the plant and continue watching other plants for pests.

No
Try a beneficial insect. You can buy them at your local nursery.

If this doesn't control the pest, ask an adult to apply an appropriate pesticide.

What is IPM?

IPM stands for "Integrated Pest Management" and is an effective way to address pest problems. Rather than applying chemical pesticides on a routine calendar basis, IPM followers make treatments only when and where monitoring shows that pest populations exceed an acceptable level, called the tolerance threshold. The various treatments are chosen and timed to be most effective on pests and least disruptive to natural controls, such as beneficial organisms. The object of an IPM program is not to totally eliminate pests, but rather to keep pest populations below levels at which they cause unacceptable damage.

Treatments are made only after a series of steps have been followed. First, information about the site, plants, potential pests and problems is gathered and studied. Monitoring is the next step. The site and plants are observed on a regular basis to that pests or problems are recognized early. As soon as a problem is spotted, an injury threshold is established. If and when the damage reaches that threshold, corrective action is taken, with the least toxic treatment option tried first. Good record keeping is critical to the success of any IPM program, so that future decisions and treatments can be based on previous experience. Evaluation is the final step. Each treatment is evaluated on its effectiveness, and any side-effects recorded.

The various treatments of a pest problem are the integrated part of IPM. There are six basic treatment strategies, as follows:

1. Plant materials are selected that are pest-resistant, support natural controls, or promote ecosystem diversity (such as native plants). The materials and the design into which they are placed should be appropriate for the climate, soil conditions, available resources, and available maintenance levels.

2. The habitat is modified to discourage harboring or feeding of pests and/or to encourage increased populations of natural predators, parasites, diseases or competitors of host organisms.

3 Human behavior is changed to include practices and attitudes. Cultural practices such as mowing, fertilizing, watering, etc., can be changed to eliminate problems. Education can change attitudes about the need for "perfect" fruits and vegetables, manicured landscapes and total elimination of pest organisms.

4 Biological controls are used against pests. This may include creating an environment that enhances existing populations of natural enemies, as well as supplementing the natural population by periodically releasing natural predators.

5 Physical control of some insect, disease and weed pests is effective for small populations. It includes handpicking, barriers, traps, water sprays and dry conditions.

6 Use chemical controls with an emphasis on those of an organic origin. There are scents that lure, repel and confuse pests; hormones that either stop pest development or act as contraceptives; fumigants; poisons that either kill on contact or after eaten; or any combination of these.

5

Activity 27:
Ladybug Lunchline

🔍 **Objective:** Determine the valuable effect of ladybugs to the garden

🕐 **Time:** 30-40 minutes

✂️ **Materials:** 1 clear film canister per child, plastic aquarium tubing or flexible drinking straws, hand-held single-hole puncher, gauze and modeling clay

NOTE: *Before beginning, do a little bit of research to find the three most common harmful garden insects for your area. You can find that information by contacting your local county Extension office, a local garden center, or speaking with a neighborhood garden expert! Use reference materials, online sources and resource links at www.jmgkids.org/wildlifegardener*

Ladybugs are considered beneficial insects; they eat insects that are harmful to our garden plants (like aphids, mealybugs and scale). Explain the concept of beneficial insects to the gardeners. Share images of your community's common garden pests. Discuss the fact that many people dislike insects and the word "insect" makes most people think of creepy, crawly, disgusting bugs. Point out that many, many insects, like ladybugs, are beneficial. In fact, tiny ladybugs can eat up to 60 aphids per day—which is a lot considering the size of a ladybug! Have students create a cumulative daily count over a two-week period of the number of aphids a ladybug could consume (day 1, 60 aphids, 2-120, 3-180, 4-240, etc.).

Bug Suckers

The white, translucent film canisters work best for this activity and can be obtained free from a local film processing office.

Tell the JMGers that they are going to be beneficial insects.

Have each person make a bug sucker by following these steps:

1. Punch one hole about halfway down the side of a film canister using a handheld hole puncher. Punch another hole across from the first.

2. Place a 1 inch piece of gauze over one of the holes and insert a 3-4 inch piece of tubing in the hole. *The gauze acts as a very important filter.*

3. Measure, cut and insert an 8-12 inch piece of tubing in the second hole and seal around the tube and hole with a small amount of modeling clay.

4. Cap the film canister.

Tell the group that they have created a bug sucker, also known as an insect aspirator. Explain that an insect aspirator is a piece of equipment that scientists use to collect insects. It's especially good for insects that are very small, very fragile, or might even be able to sting such as an ant.

Take the group outside with their bug suckers. Tell everyone that they are going to try to be beneficial to plants like a ladybug. They should try to "eat"

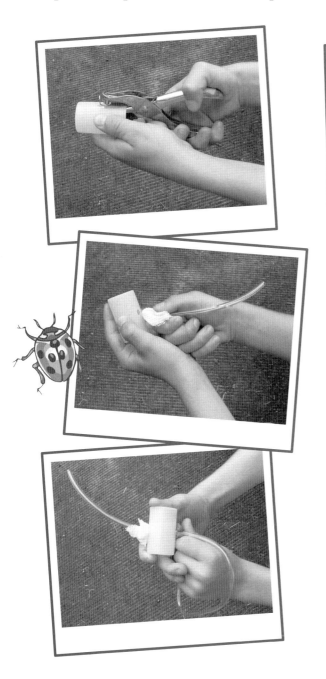

as many insects as they can by sucking them through the tubing into the film canister. But, they should be sure to "eat" only harmful insects. Give the group 5-10 minutes to "eat" insects. Discuss some basic safety rules such as to be careful to avoid stinging insects (it's a bad idea to stick a bug sucker near an ant bed!)

Afterwards, go back inside and inspect the insects that have been collected. Count how many harmful insects each person has "eaten." Remind the group of the fact that a ladybug, roughly the size of of one of their fingernails, can consume 60 aphids in one day – a natural pest control!

If needed, revisit reference materials and online resources at _www.jmgkids.org/ wildlifegardener_ to identify any unknown captured insects and to find out if they are harmful or beneficial in the garden.

In the Classroom

Tell the group that they are each going to write a special poem about ladybugs. The poems should include descriptions of what they observed when they watched the ladybugs.

Explain that haiku is a form of Japanese poetry.
Write the rules for a haiku on a chalkboard or poster board.

- A haiku consists of 3 lines

- The first line contains 5 syllables

- The second line contains 7 syllables

- The third line contains 5 syllables

Ask each person to watch a few ladybugs or look at pictures of ladybugs and write his/her own haiku. Ask for illustrations as well. Afterwards, have everyone read his poem to the group.

Example Ladybug Haiku:

Spotted ladybug,   *(5 syllables)*
Half-circle eating aphids,   *(7 syllables)*
Friend to my garden.   *(5 syllables)*

Wildlife:
Reptiles &
Amphibians

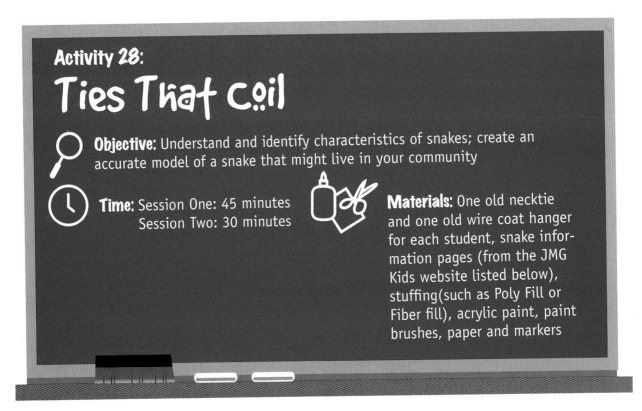

Activity 28:
Ties That Coil

Objective: Understand and identify characteristics of snakes; create an accurate model of a snake that might live in your community

Time: Session One: 45 minutes
Session Two: 30 minutes

Materials: One old necktie and one old wire coat hanger for each student, snake information pages (from the JMG Kids website listed below), stuffing(such as Poly Fill or Fiber fill), acrylic paint, paint brushes, paper and markers

 NOTE: *Before leading this activity, visit the resource links at www.jmgkids.org/wildlifegardener to identify and print out photos and descriptions of snakes common to your area. Print out enough of the snake information pages so each student has his own copy. If a computer lab area is available, students should locate, select and print the snake information pages themselves.*

Before presenting this lesson, follow the directions on page 108 to make your own necktie snake model. Anytime someone mentions the word snake, there are usually at least a few people in the room that will say that they are terrified of them. At a younger age these fears can usually be tamed a bit by correcting misinformation about the reclusive reptiles. This activity will familiarize your students with sizes and markings of snakes that are common to your area while teaching them the benefits snakes provide to a garden setting. In addition, students will learn to be cautious in places these animals are likely to be and to keep them at a distance even though very few of the snakes they are likely to see will be poisonous.

Introduce your sample snake to the group by sharing what kind of snake it is, what it likes to eat, where it lives, etc. Explain that many people are afraid of snakes and would probably try to kill any snake they ever saw. Tell the group that before you ask their opinions about snakes, they are going to learn about and become experts on snakes that live in their area. They are also going to be making one of the snakes that might be living in their community. Briefly explain the process by which they'll be making their snake model. Explain that before they can begin making the model they have to collect data about the snake they will be learning about. Have the students complete a copy of Native Snake Statistics, page 110. Once the data has been collected, they can begin work on their "Ties that Coil" models.

Ugly Tie Day!

To collect enough neck ties for this activity, have an "Ugly Tie Day" with your group! A week before the lesson invite your JMGers to wear or bring in an ugly tie. The ties can be old and unwanted ties donated from dad's, a neighbor's or an uncle's closet. On Ugly Tie Day, write each student's name on the back of the tie with a permanent marker and then lay them out for a contest. Create different categories, like Most Colorful, Most Unusual, and of course, Most Ugly. If possible, encourage students to bring in additional ties in case others aren't able to get one.

6

Necktie Snake Models

1 Measuring from the thinner end of the tie, cut the tie to the actual length of the snake plus two inches (for space to close the opening later).

 The day before this activity, squeeze a line of school glue along the stitching on the back of the tie to secure the seam.

2 Lay the tie flat and tape town the ends. Use paints and brushes to create markings on the front of the tie to match the markings on the back of the snake. TIP: It is a good idea to allow students to paint one layer and let it dry before painting over or along side with patterns of a different color. Once the back of the snake is dry, flip it over to paint the belly of the snake.

3 Unwind the coat hanger and straighten the wire. Bend the wire and fold over at one point so that it is slightly shorter than the length of the snake and insert the wire into the sleeve of the tie.

4 Using your fingers and the eraser end of a pencil, push bits of the stuffing into the openings so the body of the snake is completely filled out.

5 Have an adult fold in the "mouth" of the snake and carefully seal the opening using hot glue.

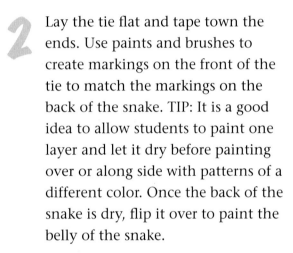

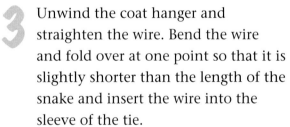

6 Once the snake has been filled out and the opening has been sealed, use paint to touch up any areas that need to be covered (especially along the side), Add details on the head and tail.

Once the detail paint has dried, have each student present his snake and share the information he learned about the snake to the rest of the group. The group should then pose the snakes in their classroom, meeting place or some area that will be visited by adults or other youths.

In the Classroom

Ask students to think about the different land types and variations in climate in which people live around the world. Have the students list each continent and as a group briefly discuss how people might live and dress differently to live there. Of course even in North America people live in extremes of hot to moderate to very cold climates, from flat plains to mammoth mountainscapes and from arid deserts to rainforest conditions, so conditions in which people live can be quite different.

Once the students have researched snakes, ask them to think about the landforms and climates in which snakes are found. Challenge them to find the only continent on which snakes are not found. For the answer to this and more information about snakes, visit *www.jmgkids.org/wildlifegardener*

Native Snake Statistics

Common Name: _____

Scientific Name: _____

Colors on Snake: _____

Patterns or Markings: _____

_____

Photo of Snake

Habitat of Snake: _____

_____

What the Snake Eats: _____

Other Special Information: _____

_____

Activity 29:
Lizard Lair

Objective: Distinguish between and understand the benefits of lizards in a garden; construct a shelter to attract lizards to a garden

Time: 45 minutes

Materials: Large clay pot (10" or larger), sticks, flat rock or small clay saucer, and golf ball to baseball-sized rocks to fill the clay pot

Lizards are found though the world. They can be some of the most interesting, colorful and beneficial additions to a garden habitat. Your JMG group can welcome lizards to your garden area by creating a Lizard Lair that provides a shelter and even a perfect place to bask in the sun.

Ask the group to describe lizards, how they look, how they act, where they live, what they eat, etc. Have the students share stories of lizards they may have come across, including what colors of lizards they have seen, how big they are, what they saw the lizard doing, etc. During the discussion, point out these cool lizard facts:

- Lizards are reptiles (they are cold-blooded and must rely on the environment to warm or cool their bodies)

- Lizards will often seek shelter in rocks, brush piles or other small, confined areas

- Some lizards can change their color to blend into their surroundings (this is a cool adaptation that has helped them to survive by being better at hiding and hunting!)

- Most lizards commonly found around the home feed on insects and spiders

- Most lizards have the ability to lose and grow back a tail (tails can be lost as they are escaping from a predator)

- Some lizards are legless

- Some lizards can chirp, squeak or make other sounds

Tell the group that they will be creating a home for lizards in their garden. Ask the group of gardeners go on a scavenger

6

hunt to look for the materials to create the garden's Lizard Lair. They will need to find:

• golf ball to baseball-sized rocks

• any rocks with a flat shape

• thick sticks.

Have students carefully place rocks and sticks in a large pot until full. Gently rock the container back and forth to settle the contents and place the container in a protected area that receives partial sunlight. Place flat stones or small clay saucer atop the rocks to create a basking stone for the lizards. Use additional rocks or sticks if needed to make a firm base for the basking stone.

Ask the group to make predictions about how effective the Lizard Lair might be in attracting more lizards to the garden

habitat. Have the students create a log of lizard sightings in the garden area on a calendar simply by placing a tally mark for each different time a lizard is spotted. Also ask students to make a note of the time of day the lizard siting took place to determine if lizards are more active during certain times of the day.

Multiple Lizard Lairs can be placed around different areas of the garden to attract larger numbers of the reptiles. Remind the group that as they work to include more components of habitat that are meeting the specific needs of specific wildlife, they are more likely to have those wildlife make a home in the garden area!

If acrylic paints are available, allow the students to decorate the Lizard Lairs!

Did You Know?

Lizards and other reptiles do not produce their own heat.
The same light and heat energy that plants and other livings need
to survive also provides the heat that lizards and other reptiles need to
allow their bodies to function. Lizards will find surfaces, like
rocks, that are warmed by the sun and will bask in
the sun to warm their bodies.

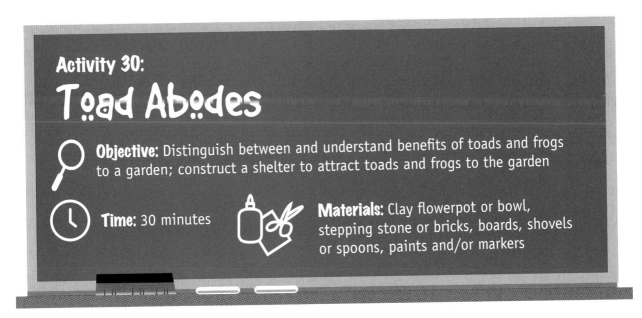

Activity 30:
Toad Abodes

Objective: Distinguish between and understand benefits of toads and frogs to a garden; construct a shelter to attract toads and frogs to the garden

Time: 30 minutes

Materials: Clay flowerpot or bowl, stepping stone or bricks, boards, shovels or spoons, paints and/or markers

Tell your JMGers that toads and frogs are friends to our gardens. Ask them if they know why. Toads and frogs eat many unwanted insects and other pests. Tell the gardeners that they are going to try to attract these garden pals by creating houses for them.

Try the following ideas. Place each Toad Abode in a shady, moist area of your habitat garden.

Clay flowerpots or bowls

Use a cracked flowerpot or large bowl. Students can use a hammer to break off a section of the top edge of the pot. This works best if the pot is laid on the ground and the piece is broken of with a strike from the inside edge of the pot. They should break off a small section about the size of a 50 cent piece. Students can decorate with paints or markers—keep in mind that the flowerpot or bowl will be turned upside down. Place them upside down in your garden.

Stepping stones or bricks

Use an old stepping stone or some bricks. Place the stepping stone or a few bricks on the ground near an outdoor water spigot or other moist area. With a shovel or spoon, dig away some of the soil under one edge of the stone or bricks. This will be the "door" of the Toad Abode. Students can decorate them with paints or markers.

Boards

Construct a house for a toad or frog using old wooden boards or blocks. Ask your gardeners to come up with a design. Have them decorate and place it in the garden. Some sample designs are shown on the next page.

Other materials

Invite your gardeners come up with and try out additional Toad Abode ideas!

6

Have the JMGers conduct an experiment to see what types of Toad Abodes are more effective than others and what types of locations are best for a Toad Abode. Have the group brainstorm ideas for an experiment. After the Toad Abodes have been in place for a week or so, have your gardeners inspect them for toads or frogs. Then ask the following questions:

- Which Toad Abode was best at attracting a toad or frog?

- Why do you think so?

- Which did not attract a toad or frog?

- Why do you think so?

In the Classroom

Is that a frog or a toad in your Toad Abode and is there a difference? Tell the group that both frogs and toads start out in very similar ways–as tadpoles looking very much like fish. Over time, they develop legs and lose their tails and gills. Then, they are able to live on land. At this point, the differences become more noticeable. Share the frog and toad facts below to help your gardeners distinguish between the mysterious hoppers.

Frogs

- Spend most of their time near water
- Smooth texture of skin
- Protruding eyes
- Longer hind legs for jumping and swimming
- Lay eggs in masses

Toads

- Spend most of their time in drier environments
- Shorter hind legs for crawling
- Bumpy and dry textured skin
- Lay eggs in long chains

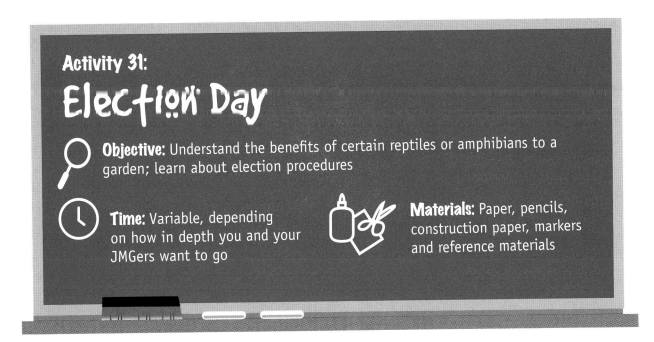

Activity 31:

Election Day

Objective: Understand the benefits of certain reptiles or amphibians to a garden; learn about election procedures

Time: Variable, depending on how in depth you and your JMGers want to go

Materials: Paper, pencils, construction paper, markers and reference materials

Ask your JMGers if they have ever voted for anything. Tell them that people can vote on all sorts of things, including who they want to represent them in political and governmental situations. Ask your JMGers for examples of positions people might vote for in an election (a president, senator, mayor, etc.). Tell the JMG group that they are going to hold an election and they will be selecting the "First Friend of the Garden."

Start by telling the group that only a reptile or amphibian can be elected to the position and that there are four candidates: frogs/toads, snakes, turtles and lizards. Have the gardeners choose which candidate they want to support. The students will form each candidate's election committee.

Next, have each group research their candidate. Ask the groups to use reference materials and links to

online resources available at *www.jmgkids.org/wildlifegardener* to find information including advantages and disadvantages of having their candidate in a garden. *The candidate research information should include:*

• the specific frog/toad, snake, turtle, lizard that will be focused on

• the habitat the candidate lives in

• the food the candidate consumes

• the benefit the candidate offers the garden

• any negatives of having the candidate in the garden

• and any other special information about the candidate

After the groups have found information, they should begin to plan the election campaign. Ask your gardeners for examples of what people do when they

6

run for office. This can include posting signs, handing out buttons or stickers, and/or meeting people. Each group can decide how they would like to campaign. The groups can make signs and/or buttons, or any other campaign paraphernalia. Set a date for other students to participate in a school-wide election.

As an option, on the election day, allow the groups to campaign for about 10-15 minutes. Each group should select one member of their election committee to give a brief presentation about why their candidate should be the "First Friend of the Garden." This member, with help of the rest of his/her committee, can address questions from voters. Allow for as much as a 10-minute question and answer period.

After these activities are completed, ask the students to vote for their choice of the "First Friend of the Garden."

Wildlife Habitat Sites

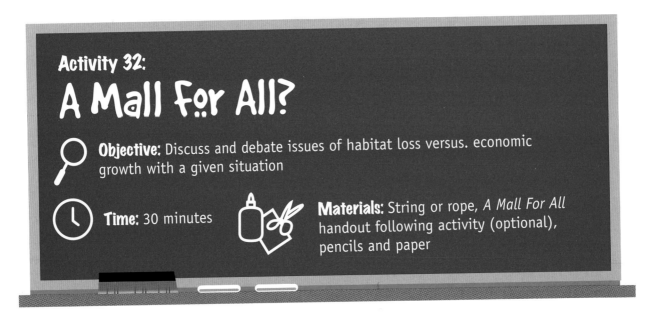

Activity 32:
A Mall For All?

Objective: Discuss and debate issues of habitat loss versus. economic growth with a given situation

Time: 30 minutes

Materials: String or rope, *A Mall For All* handout following activity (optional), pencils and paper

You are going to tell your gardeners a story about a problem that is occurring in a town nearby. Explain to the group that they are going to pretend that they live in this town. Read or make handouts of the following background information to the group.

The Habitat

There is a park-like area in the town called Arbor Ridge Forest. It is a beautiful, densely wooded area that many of the town's residents like to visit. Many animals make their homes here. Rabbits and deer eat leaves and stems from many of the plants found here. Squirrels climb the trees and gather nuts. Beautiful butterflies are constantly moving from flower to flower, drinking nectar. Many birds build nests in the trees and their songs can be heard throughout the day. At night, bats fly around and catch insects and owls hoot in the trees. People regularly exercise by walking in these woods and enjoy watching the animals and listening to the birds. One family had a picnic there yesterday and they even saw a deer and her fawn!

The Shopping Mall

This is a medium-sized town and there is no place to shop. When someone wants to shop for a new pair of shoes, clothes or anything besides groceries, they have to go to the mall in the next town. It takes over an hour to drive there. It isn't convenient to shop at this mall since it is far away, but there is no other choice. It is an especially big problem every year around the holidays and when school starts because everyone in this town drives to the next town to shop. The roadway gets very crowded and the traffic makes the shopping trip take much longer. Many people wish that their town had a mall of its own and are very excited to hear the rumors that there may be a new, large mall on the way. And now the residents of this town are starting to see billboards advertising the possibility of a new mall and all of the great stores and new jobs that will come with it!

The Situation

Recently, the town council announced there is a company was interested in building a shopping mall in the area. The town council had a meeting a few days ago with a construction business that planning to build the mall. The only area in town large enough to accommodate the mall is the Arbor Ridge Forest area of town. Many people have seen the billboards and are excited about all of the new businesses and many jobs that will come to their town but know that the ads don't mention the habitat area will be removed. Many others, however, don't like this plan at all. They don't want the woods to be destroyed. They understand that if most of the habitat is removed, most of the animals will not be able to live there. Both sides have been arguing about this issue since the town council announced the plan to allow the mall to be built.

Tell the groups that the town council wants to be fair. The council has decided to hold a special meeting so that people on both sides of the issue can express their opinions. Tell the groups that they are going to participate in the town meeting. Use string to divide the room into two sections. Tell the group that one section is for everyone who favors building the shopping mall and the other section is for everyone who wants to leave the forest as it is. Ask the gardeners to count off (1,2,1,2,1,2...) and have all the ones sit in on 'the building the new mall' side and all the twos sitting on the 'keeping the wooded area' side.

Ask them to think about the situation and decide on reasons why their position is right. Each group should select one person to be their spokesperson, or individual students can take turns speaking for their group. Have one person start the debate by stating a reason why they believe their side's opinion is correct. A second student from the other point of view then gets to respond. Continue the debate, allowing the groups to respond to one another until several from each side have stated all of their points.

Once several points have been made for both sides, ask the groups the following questions: Does the town need a shopping mall? Does the town need the wooded area? Should the mall be built, or should the woods be preserved?

7

Throughout this activity, it is likely this debate discussion will get lively – even elementary-aged students can have strong opinions about such issues. The lesson is not about which side can win the argument, but to have both sides hear each other's points and understand there is more than one side to such an issue.

Allow each side to make one final point. Once both groups are finished, explain that there is no correct answer to this situation. Tell them that problems often have no easy answers; they must decide for themselves what is right and what should be done.

At this point, remove the string dividing the groups. Tell them that now they are not two groups each trying to win but now will work together. Ask the two groups if this is an issue that both sides could come to some agreement on. Challenge the groups to each come up with a compromise solution. Have each side spend 10 minutes talking about a solution to the problem that they think both sides would be happy with. Remind the groups to think about the points the other side made as they try to come up with a solution. When time is up, allow both group a few minutes to present their ideas to the other group.

In the Classroom

Have each student write a letter to the city council. They have two options of the type of letter they can write. Their first option is to write a persuasive letter arguing their original point of view to the city council. The second option is to write and propose their best compromise solution.

A Mall for All?

The Habitat

There is a park-like area in the town called Arbor Ridge Forest. It is a beautiful, densely wooded area that many of the town's residents like to visit. Many animals make their homes there. Rabbits and deer eat leaves and stems from many of the plants found there. Squirrels climb the trees and gather nuts. Beautiful butterflies constantly move from flower to flower, drinking nectar. Many birds build nests in the trees and their chirping can be heard throughout the day. At night, bats fly around and catch insects and owls hoot in the trees. People regularly walk in these woods and watch the animals and listen to the birds. A family had a picnic there yesterday and they even saw a deer and her fawn!

The Shopping Mall

This is a medium-sized town and there is no place to shop. When someone wants to shop for a new pair of shoes, clothes or anything besides groceries, they have to go to the mall in the next town. It takes over an hour to drive there. It isn't convenient to shop at this mall because it is far away, but there is no other choice. It is an especially big problem every year when it is time for school to start and around the holidays; everyone in this town drives to the next town to shop. The roadway gets very crowded and the traffic makes the shopping trip take much longer. Many people wish that their town had a mall of its own and are very excited to hear a rumor that there may be a new, large mall on the way!

The Situation

Recently, the town council announced that there was a company that was wanting to build a shopping mall in the area. The town council had a meeting a few days ago with a construction business that will build the mall. The only area in town large enough to accommodate the mall is the Arbor Ridge Forest area of town. Many people are excited about all of the new businesses that will come to their town. All of these businesses will provide jobs for many, many people. Many others, however, don't like this plan at all. They don't want the woods to be destroyed. They wonder where all of the animals will live if their habitat is destroyed. Both sides have been arguing about this issue since the town council announced the plan to build the mall.

7

Activity 33:
Mini-Meadow

Objective: Create a small meadow to attract wildlife

Time: Variable

Materials: Tape measure, trash bags, *Mini-Meadow Site Survey, Mini-Meadow Data page, Before and After page,* pencils, crayons, paper and wildflower seeds

Ask the group if they have ever walked through a meadow. Have the group help you describe a meadow. Students likely will think of an open, sunny, grassy area with butterflies and birds fluttering through the area. Have the group close their eyes and imagine being in a meadow and have them think about how they might feel if they were walking through. Give them several minutes to draw a picture of what they see in their minds.

As the name Mini-Meadow implies, a successful meadow area can be quite small. Even an eight foot square bed can make a great Mini-Meadow that can provide food and shelter for your garden habitat!

Tell the group that they will be creating a Mini-Meadow. The meadow will be a place they will be able to enjoy and it will grow and bloom year after year. Point out that even a Mini-Meadow can attract wildlife because it provides many components of basic habitat. The thick growth of flowers and grasses can provide shelter, a food source and an area for insects and other small animals to raise young. Explain that it will be a small area that will take some time to create but their patience will pay off as the meadow grows.

The group will have to think about and select an area of land that has certain qualities. Make a list of each of the following features and discuss the terms and what each means:

- An open area with full sun

- An area with well-drained soil

- An area with that can go unmowed

Have the group brainstorm and record a list of possible sites in the immediate area for the meadow. To narrow the list down, have the group vote on their top three choices of possible locations. Provide each student with a copy of the *Mini-Meadow Site Survey* and take the group out to evaluate the appropriateness of each location. Once all of the sites are surveyed, have the group review the survey forms and rank/rate each site on a scale. This will probably spark discussions and debates. Write the rank/rating on the appropriate line and use the rating to determine the best location.

Once the location has been selected, the group should begin planning a planting and seeding time. The group will need to determine the following:

1. What to plant and when plant it.

3. How they will obtain plants/seed.

4 How they will plant.

5. How the area will be maintained

Once the components of the plan are in place, they will have the information they need to plan how they will get permission.

What to Plant

As your group selects plants for their Mini-Meadow, there are many options for creating a dense growth of grasses, wildflowers and other plants that can provide the components of habitat. Using plants that are native to your area is always a good idea. Native plants are adapted well to a given area and will generally do well with very little extra care.

Wildflowers can also be a good choice within a mini-meadow. These hardy blooming plants also create a dense source of growth with vibrant splashes of seasonal color and serve as a nectar and pollen source for pollinators. Call the local county Extension agent, garden center, or nursery professional and ask for a list of recommended native plants or wildflowers for your area. More information about regional native plants or wildflowers can be found online through resource links at *www.jmgkids.org/wildlifegardener*.

When to Plant

Native plants grown in pots can be transplanted year round but the best time to plant is early spring. Generally, most wildflowers in the western and southern United States do best when the seeds are planted in the fall and those in the northern and northeastern areas of the country should be sown in early spring. For more information, visit the resources available at: *www.jmgkids.org/wildlifegardener*

obtaining Plants and Seeds

Obtaining native plants and wildflowers for the Mini-Meadow can be an opportunity to have students use their persuasive writing skills to ask local

7

businesses for donations to help your JMG group grow the meadow. Students should include in their letters who they are, what they want to do, why they want to do it, and specifically how that business can help. Fundraising efforts asking each business for funds to purchase a few packets of seed or a single native plant can also be very successful.

How to Plant Seeds

The easiest way to plant wildflower seeds is to simply scatter the seed by throwing it out over the area. You will greatly increase your chances for success by increasing the amount of seed that actually comes in contact with the soil. If you will be planting in an area of thick growth of grass or weeds the seed to soil contact can be improved The more of the following steps that can be taken to prepare the soil, the more dramatic the results will be:

1. mow the area as short as possible

2. as an option, the area can be sprayed with an approved herbicide

3. rake away grass or weeds to expose more soil (Very thick grassy areas may even be tilled lightly to break up the top layer of sod.)

Once the area has been prepared, the seeds can be cast. Your young gardeners will enjoy throwing the seed. Before the seed can be distributed, it should be mixed with sand or potting soil. This helps the seeds to be distributed more evenly. Have students take a "wildflower

walk" and step over the entire area to press the seeds into the soil.

When time comes to clear the area for planting, solicit the support of parents and volunteers. This is a great way to establish support and ownership of the project among a larger group!

Did You Know?

One handful of wildflower seed can contain enough seed for thousands of plants. It is important to mix seed with a "carrier" such as sand or potting soil to help ensure that seeds will be planted with enough room to grow.

Maintaining the Area

For the first few weeks following planting, the area will need to be moistened to help the plants and seedlings become established. If adequate rainfall is not available, light watering may be necessary.

Maintenance of the Mini-Meadow area includes *not mowing*. As the area grows and fills in, some weeds may begin to infiltrate the meadow area. When this happens, your group of gardeners can decide whether or not the weed should stay or go. Explain that a weed is just an undesirable plant. In many cases, students will decide to allow weeds to stay. If students decide a weed should go or if the weed begins to overgrow plants around it, have the group periodically work to pull the unwanted plants.

Getting Permission

If your group decides to plant on school grounds or any public area, permission will need to be obtained first. Before seeking approval for a project like this, it is best to have all of the above questions thought through and answered. Be sure the person who is granting permission knows that the area will be a protected, unmowed area.

Once a site is selected, students will need to measure the dimensions of the area. The group can measure the length and multiply by the width to determine the area of the meadow. This will be important when determining the amount of seed and/or number of plants needed for the meadow. Have students practice

measuring in both yards and meters and record the measurements on their *Mini-Meadow Data* page, page 128.

After planting, record what types of seeds were sown and transplants were installed on the *Mini-Meadow Data* page. Afterwards, ask the group to predict what the meadow will look like. Periodically take the group out to observe their meadow. Have them record what they see on the *Before and After* page, page 129.

Although a true meadow can take a few years to mature, your group will be able to start enjoying the Mini-Meadow in a matter of weeks.

For additional information about creating your Mini-Meadow, visit resource links at: *www.jmgkids.org/wildlifegardener*

7

In the Classroom

If your group plants wildflowers and they have grown in, have students each pick one flower to preserve and to create a *Wildflower Bio*. Ideally each type of wildflower in the meadow will be represented from all of those selected by the students. Flowers can be pressed and dried by placing several sheets of newspaper on a piece of cardboard. Place a paper towel on top of the newspaper. Arrange the flowers so that the leaves and blooms are lying as flat as possible on the paper towel. Put another paper towel on top of the flowers. Cover it with more newspaper and another piece of cardboard. Stack a few heavy books on top. The flowers will be preserved and ready for mounting in 10-14 days.

Flowers should be mounted by carefully brushing a very thin layer of glue onto the page and gently laying the pressed flower onto the glued area. Have students fill in data for each *Wildflower Bio* page. Compile all mounted flowers into a single book by stapling or punching holes in each biography page and tying each all of them together with colorful yarn. You can also have students complete a *Biography Of...* page (page 130) of other members of the JMG group to include info about the group that contributed to the Wildflower Bio Book.

Mini-Meadow Site Survey

Name: _____

You are trying to decide on the best place to grow a wildflower meadow. Circle one number for each line, with 5 meaning "best" and 1 meaning "worst".

Location of Site 1: _____

Area has full sunlight	1	2	3	4	5
Area has well drained soil	1	2	3	4	5
Small plants and grasses are growing in the area	1	2	3	4	5

Add up all of the numbers in the box above and write the answer in the star.

What was that site's score?

Location of Site 1: _____

Area has full sunlight	1	2	3	4	5
Area has well drained soil	1	2	3	4	5
Small plants and grasses are growing in the area	1	2	3	4	5

Add up all of the numbers in the box above and write the answer in the star.

What was that site's score?

Location of Site 1: _____

Area has full sunlight	1	2	3	4	5
Area has well drained soil	1	2	3	4	5
Small plants and grasses are growing in the area	1	2	3	4	5

Add up all of the numbers in the box above and write the answer in the star.

What was that site's score?

Which site had the highest score?   1   2   3

7

Meadow Data

Draw the shape of the meadow within the box below.

1. Measure the length of each straight side of the meadow and write the measurement beside each straight line in your picture above. (If the area is too large, use a separate sheet of graph paper)

2. How many square feet are in the meadow area?_____

3. On the back of this page, list the types of native plants or wildflower seeds planted.

Meadow Before and After

Before *(Today's Date)* _____

1. Describe what the site looks like now.

_____

_____

Wildlife Clues

2. List and draw pictures of wildlife you have seen
   or clues that wildlife has been in this area (such
   as animal tracks, leaves that have been chewed,
   or a spider web).

Insects _____, _____, _____

Birds _____, _____, _____

Other Small animals _____, _____

3. Do you think the Mini-Meadow will attract wildlife? What animals?

_____

4. Draw a picture of what the area looks like and staple it to this page.

After *(Today's Date)* _____

1. Go back and read your description of what the
   area looked like before it was a meadow.
   Describe what it looks like now.

_____

_____

Wildlife Clues

2. List and draw pictures of wildlife you have seen
   or clues that wildlife has been in this area

Insects _____, _____, _____

Birds _____, _____, _____

Other Small animals _____, _____

3. Draw a picture of what the area looks like and staple it to this page.

Biography of...

Name _____

Date of Birth _____

Birthplace _____

Height _____

Eye Color _____

Hair Color _____

Number of brothers and/or sisters _____

Favorite food _____

Favorite color _____

Favorite things to do _____

Now use this information to write a paragraph about this person!

_____

_____

_____

_____

_____

_____

_____

Wildflower Bio

Name of Flower _____

Height _____

Width _____

Bloom Color _____

Glue flower here

Personal Information

This flower grows in a _____ (type of habitat).

It likes the _____ (sun or shade).

_____ _____ (type of insect) **like this flower.**

The plant this flower grows on is _____ (how tall or wide).

The leaves are _____ (describe the leaves).

I like this flower because _____

_____

What are some interesting things that you noticed about this flower?

_____

_____

_____

_____

7

Activity 34:

Recycled Water Garden

Objective: Design and create a mini aquatic habitat by building a container water garden

Time: Variable, depending on the complexity of the design

Materials: Recycled container of almost any sort (if container is not watertight, water sealing spray, or other water sealer or liner will need to be used), plants, sterile pea gravel, fertilizer tablets and *Before and After* worksheet

NOTE: You can attract more wildlife with a larger pond, but container water gardens have the advantage of being less expensive and much easier to assemble. Container water gardens may attract dragonflies, bees, butterflies, and songbirds. Small fish and snails can also be introduced to a container garden.

Many of the youths in your group have likely worked in a vegetable garden, flower bed, or even a habitat garden area, but ask the gardeners if they have ever worked in a *water* garden. Explain that there are many plants that grow in and underwater in oceans, lakes, rivers and even in ditches. Life in bodies of water and even along shorelines could not exist without the most basic plants such as algae and other water plants. These plants serve as the foundation of the food chain and pump oxygen into the water.

On a much smaller scale, your group can create a container water garden. Tell the group that they will be constructing a water garden in a container that will become a miniature ecosystem of living plants and animals. Almost any container can be used. It is best if your container is at least 10-12" deep as it will be easier to find plants for your garden.

First, brainstorm with the group a list of possible containers – encourage them to think creatively. They should consider anything that is an open-topped container that can be recycled as a container water garden. To get the group thinking in the right direction, start off the list with ideas such as a broken wheelbarrow, old clay pot, metal tub, an old sink, etc. If needed, assign the gardeners homework of looking around their homes for new ideas and bringing at least one additional idea to add to the list.

Once a container is decided on, take the group on a walk around the building to look for an area where a water garden could be placed. The garden will be successful anywhere it can receive full sun (at least 6-8 hours of sun per day).

Your container must be watertight. If it is not, you need to seal it. Use a polyurethane spray to coat the inside of a porous container or use silicon to fill cracks. Another very easy option is to purchase a section of pond liner. Liners can be purchased by the foot at most home improvement stores. Lay the liner into the container so that it covers the bottom and sides. Have the JMGers help fill the container half full to hold the liner in place and then cut away the excess liner along the top. Allow the container to sit for 24 hours to allow the chlorine in the container to dissipate.

The next step is for students to look for plants to add to the garden. Share with the group about the three main aquatic plant types below. Have the group visit *www.jmgkids.org/wildlifegardener* to view a gallery of aquatic plants. Each student can create a wish list of the plants they would like to include in the water garden. Have the students vote on the top three favorite plants for each category. Use this student wish list when selecting plants for purchase at a local garden center. If the container is large enough, include different plant types.

Submerged
Submerged plants remain below the surface of the water. They provide hiding places for small aquatic animals and help oxygenate the water.

Floating
Floating plants help shade the water, which cools the water and controls algae. Floating plants should cover about half of the water's surface.

Emergent
Emergent plants grow above the water surface. They can provide hiding places for wildlife and may provide a place for insects to perch and emerge.

Place the plants in the water garden container, and if possible keep the plants in their original pots. Inquire at the location of purchase if your plants require fertilizer. It is likely that specific fertilizer tablets may need to be added to the water or in the pots of your aquatic plants. Complete filling the container with water.

7

If your container is large enough, have your gardeners create a small shelf to establish a deep area and a shallow area. These levels can be created simply by stacking bricks at different heights in the container. An attractive option after planting all of the plants is to cover the soil with pea gravel. Students should add water as needed to keep the water level constant.

Send out your creative ideas for your group's Recycled Water Garden! Send a description of your Recycled Water Garden and tell us how you made it and how you got the idea along with a picture. Selected images will be posted at the Recycled Water Garden Gallery at the JMG Website! For information on submitting your idea, go to: *www.jmgkids.org/wildlifegardener*

In the Classroom

Have the students closely observe the aquatic plants in your group's garden. If possible, have them take the plant from the container and examine with a magnifying glass. Ask them to look for anything unusual – anything that makes them different from regular, terrestrial plants.

Point out that water plants are especially adapted to live in the aquatic environment. Ask the students to think about how plant would have to be different from plants that grow on land.

What did the students notice when examining that plants? Although all plants are different, some interesting aquatic plant adaptations are described below.

- Because water plants are normally supported by water, they lack the structure that causes them to "stand" (this is why most water plants are limp when removed from water)

- The flexible structure of these plants allows them to be bend with water movement. Plants growing in areas of a great deal of water movement often have leaves and stems rubbery and ribbon-like that allows them to move easily in the current

- Aquatic plants often grow bubble-like air-filled cavities in their leaves and stems that help to hold the plant up

- Land plants have a protective layer over the leaves that prevents the leaves from losing water. Aquatic plants don't have such a layer. (these plants will often dry out quickly when removed from water)

- Roots do very little absorbing of nutrients, water and oxygen instead they mostly serve to anchor the plant

- Some aquatic plants have no anchoring and float along wherever the current carries them! This allows new plants to grow and be carried over great distances

Point out that just like all living things, plants are made up of systems that help the plant live and grow and reproduce. Discuss how each one of the listed adaptations serve a particular function and what might happen to the plant if that part of the system were removed.

7

Activity 35:
A La Carte Garden

Objective: Design a habitat garden and select plant material to attract various types of wildlife

Time: Variable, depending on your garden design and the number of participants

Materials: Plants, shovels, mulch, water for plants

 NOTE: This activity is complimented by P.L.A.N.T. and Wildlife Needs on page 2, which helps select the location of the site.

Do your young gardeners like the idea of having birds and butterflies flying through the garden? How about regular visits from a big toad or brightly-colored lizards? Listed on the following pages are several types of wildlife your group may want to attract. The group can add to an existing garden area or work to create a new space. As your group works to select a site, note that many of the components of a habitat may be maximized simply by choosing a location that already offers some of these features. For example, there already may be an area near by that has a cedar tree or that has a moist area near a water spigot.

Have the JMGers study the future habitat site and complete the "Before" section of the *Before and After* page following this activity. Have your students vote to select the wildlife they would like to see in their garden. The group can then choose at least one item from the food, water, and shelter carts to place in the garden area.

Birds

Food cart

Trees
Ash
Agarito
Bald Cypress
American Holly
Cedar/Junipers
Yaupon Holly
Prairie Grasses
Dogwood
Elms

Hummingbird plants
Flame Acanthus
Trumpet Creeper
Honeysuckle
Turk's Cap
Salvia

Shrubs
Hackberry
Viburnum
Hawthorns
Wax Myrtle
Elderberry
Crabapples
Oak
Persimmon
Pine

Other Food
Bird feeders

Water cart

Bird Bath
Overturned garbage can lid
Water garden/pond

Saucer from a large flowerpot
Fountain

Shelter cart

Wooden birdhouse
Dense brush
Gourd birdhouse
Layered plant growth

Thick shrubs
Prairie Grasses

7

Butterflies

food cart

For larva

Parsley
Dill
Hibiscus
Passionflower
Hollyhock
Salvia
Nettle

Sunflower
Willow
Milkweed
Violet
Wild Senna
Elm

For adult butterflies

Buttonbush
Passionflower
Hibiscus
Salvia
Hollyhock
Sunflower

Lantana
Verbena
Milkweed
Zinnia
Marigold
Salvia

Water cart

Shallow edge of a pond/water garden
Birdbath, shallowly filled
Flower pot saucer, shallowly filled
Mud puddle

Shelter cart

Brush pile
Tall shrubs, perennials, etc.
Tall ornamental grass
Rocks and tree trunks for basking

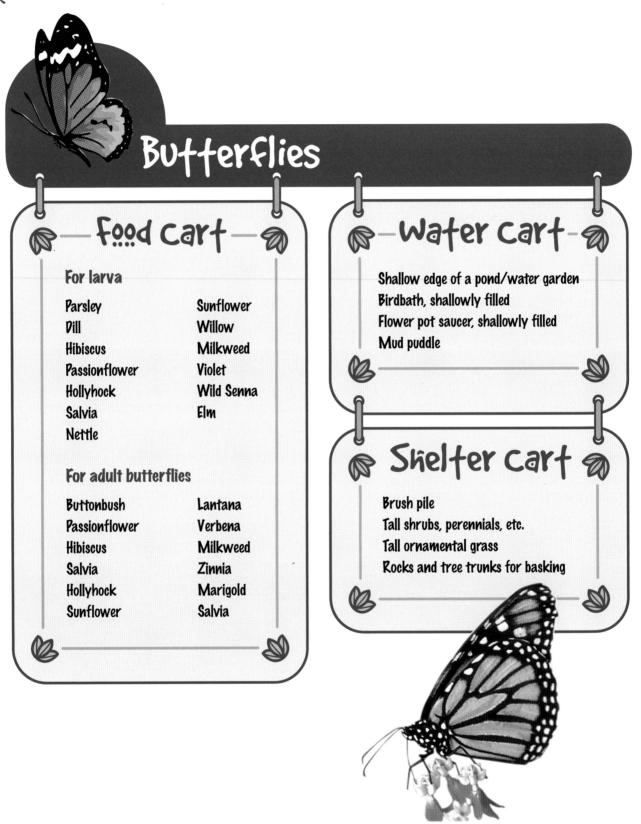

Squirrels

Food cart

Bald Cypress	Elms
Maples	Persimmon
Crabapples	Hawthorns
Oaks	Pines
Dogwood	Junipers
Pecan	Yaupon
Holly	

Water cart

Edge of a pond/water garden
Flower pot saucer
Birdbath
Overturned garbage can lid

Shelter cart

Shrubs	Trees
Snags	Brush piles
A dying tree	

7

Frogs and Toads

Food Cart

Beetles   Moths
Many pests/insects   Crickets
Slugs   Flies
Snails

Water Cart

Edge of a pond/water garden
Any area that remains moist.
Moist areas near faucets.

Shelter Cart

Brush piles   Leaf litter
Tree stumps   Fallen logs
Rock crevices

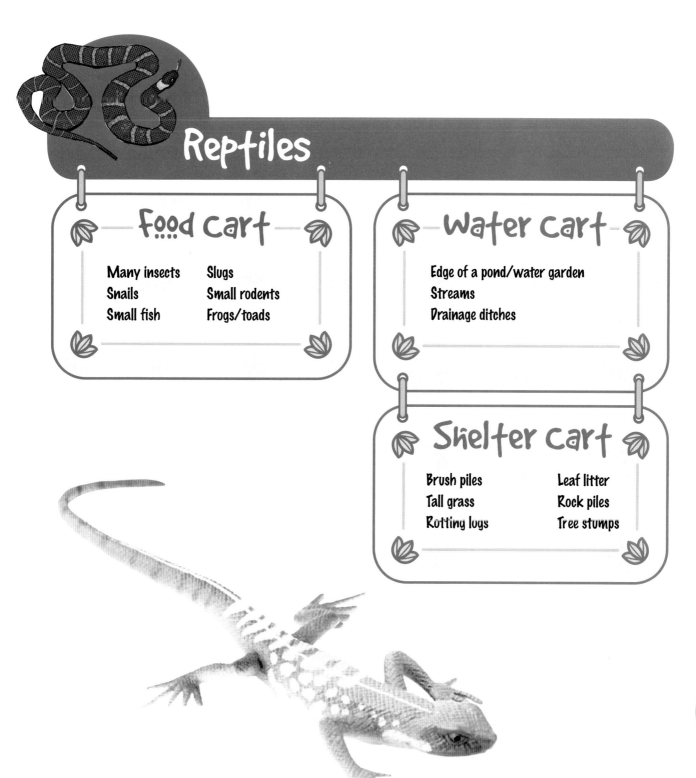

Reptiles

Food Cart

Many insects   Slugs
Snails   Small rodents
Small fish   Frogs/toads

Water Cart

Edge of a pond/water garden
Streams
Drainage ditches

Shelter Cart

Brush piles   Leaf litter
Tall grass   Rock piles
Rotting logs   Tree stumps

7

141

Once a garden site is decided on, guide the gardeners to discuss the following questions:

1. How they will obtain the materials?

2. Where to place items?

3. When they will plant?

4. How the area will be maintained?

5. How they will get permission?

obtaining Materials

Materials for the habitat may need to be purchased or donated. Many items on the lists may be available through students bringing items from home, such as a garbage can lid for a water source or bag of leaves to create leaf litter. Make sure they ask their parent or guardian for permission to donate the item to the garden.

For other items, such as small trees, bird feeders, etc., consider having students practice their persuasive writing skills by asking local businesses for support in helping your JMG group create a habitat garden. Students should include in their letters who they are, what they want to do, why they want to do it, and how that business can help. Fundraising efforts asking each business to make a small donation to fund a specific plant or other item can be very successful. Call the local county Extension agent to confirm if a listed tree or other plant can do well in your area.

Where to Place Items (Make a Garden Wall Map!)

Once all materials have been decided on, list them on the chalkboard or poster. Include in that list existing components such as trees, shrubs, rocks, etc. First, have students measure the length of the boundaries of the site of your A la Carte Garden On an open wall, begin your Garden Wall Map by using masking tape to establish the boundaries of the area that will serve at the garden habitat site. Designate a scale for your map. (Depending on the size of the wall space available, it could be 1 yard of A la Carte Garden = 1 foot on wall map). Next assign a specific item(s) that each child should add to the map. The group should make the symbols using different colors of construction paper. Help students estimate the actual size of the item and then create it to the same scale. Label each symbol and place a loop of masking tape on the back to stick it to the map.

First tape the existing component symbols to an open wall. Discuss where the group thinks each item could be located in the garden as you have students place the new symbols on the map. Once the placement of these items has been discussed and consensus is reached, be sure to have students make a sketch of the garden area.

When to Plant

Set a habitat construction date on which your JMG group plans to have available all the materials that have been brought from home or donated. Place the gardeners into small groups of 2-3 and put them in charge of planting and placing a specific item being brought in to the area. If the area is a larger size, requires additional help to till, to remove areas of sod, or to move in larger amounts of soil, elicit the support of parents and volunteers. This is a great way to establish support and ownership of the project among a larger group! See *Planning a Garden Work Day* (page 187).

Maintaining the Area

If adequate rainfall is not available, regular watering of the new plantings may be necessary.

Use the *Schedule It* activity (page 12) to assign specific students certain dates that they will be responsible for watering, weeding and fertilizing.

Getting Permission

If your group decides to plant on school grounds or any public area, you need to first obtain permission. Before seeking approval for a project like this, it is best to have all of the above questions thought through and answered.

After the area has had several weeks to gradually becomes established, have students study the area regularly to check for any signs of wildlife living in or visiting the site. After the habitat area has been in place for four to six weeks, have the JMGers compare the garden site before and after the building of their garden. Use the *A la Carte Garden: Before and After* worksheet.

A Garden Wall Map is a kid-friendly way to involve the whole group in creating a plan for the area while providing a better understanding of the importance of mapping items to scale.

A La Carte Garden Before and After

Before *(Today's Date)* _____

1. Describe what the site looks like now.

_____

_____

2. List and draw pictures of wildlife you have seen
   or clues that wildlife has visited this area (such
   as animal tracks, leaves that have been chewed,
   or a spider web).

Insects _____, _____, _____

Birds _____, _____, _____

Other Small animals _____, _____

3. Do you think the garden will attract wildlife? What animals?

_____

4. Draw a picture of what the area looks like and staple it to this page.

Wildlife Clues

After *(Today's Date)* _____

1. Go back and read your description of what the
   area looked like before it was a garden.
   Describe what it looks like now.

_____

_____

2. List and draw pictures of wildlife you have seen
   or clues that wildlife has visited this area

Insects _____, _____, _____

Birds _____, _____, _____

Other Small animals _____, _____

3. Draw a picture of what the area looks like and staple it to this page.

Wildlife Clues

Activity 36:
Backyard Buddy

Objective: Recognize individuals in the community who use environmentally friendly practices

Time: 20 minutes

Materials: *Backyard Buddy Checklist, Backyard Buddy Award* and pencils

Ask your students if they like when people tell them they have done a good job. Ask them if they would like to receive an award for doing a job well.

Tell your gardeners that they are going to have the special task of rewarding people who they know that are doing a good job. Show them the Backyard Buddy Award. Explain that this is an award given to those who take special care of the environment in their own backyard or neighborhood.

Distribute copies of the *Backyard Buddy Checklist*. Have each student make a list of people they know that might be eligible for such an award. Explain that anyone they know that earns over 90 points can receive the award. Their job is to talk to people they know that they think might be eligible for this award and ask them questions from the checklist.

Ask the group to think about their friends and family. Have them guess what

fraction of all the people they interview will earn the Backyard Buddy Award.

Go through the list to make sure the students understand what each question is asking and why it is being asked. Instruct them to go out and find at least two people that score over 90 points. Have the children sign and award certificates to those individuals. Make a list at your JMG meeting place of all the Backyard Buddies that were recognized by your group. Have your students leave a copy of the *Backyard Buddy Checklist* for those people in your community that don't score over 90 points, to give those people a chance to live a little more earth-friendly.

When the group meets again, determine the fraction of people that earned the Backyard Buddy Award. For example: the class interviewed 72 people and 14 of those interviewed earned the award, (14/72 or 7/36 or about 1/5)

7

Show the group how to convert that number to a percentage (14 ÷ 72 = 0.19, then move the decimal two places to the right, 19%). Ask the group if they were surprised by that number. Was is higher or lower than they guessed? Do they think that a lot of people could use help learning more about how to be a Backyard Buddy?

It is likely that the students will over estimate the numbers of people they know that are using all the plant and wildlife-friendly practices highlighted in this survey. Tell the group that part of their responsibility as Wildlife Gardeners and Junior Master Gardeners is to teach people around them. Remind them that they should always try to help others and to share what they know with others, but the best way to make a difference is to work hard to use these plant and wildlife-friendly practices themselves. Distribute copies of the Backyard Buddy Award certificate to be delivered to award recipients. Color copies of Backyard Buddy Award certificates can be downloaded and printed from: *www.jmgkids.org/wildlifegardener*

In the Classroom

Have students write a press release about what the group has been doing in their Junior Master Gardener study as Wildlife Gardeners. Students can write about the group's work to teach and recognize others as Backyard Buddies and include names of the award recipients. Mail the press releases to the local media – you may be surprised by the positive attention it brings your group!

Backyard Buddy Checklist

Name _____ **Date** _____

Person being interviewed _____

	Yes	No
Do you maintain a water source for birds or other wildlife?	☐ (10 points)	☐ (0 points)
Do you maintain a food source for birds or other wildlife?	☐ (10 points)	☐ (0 points)
Do you provide a birdhouse or other shelter for wildlife?	☐ (10 points)	☐ (0 points)
Are a variety of plants available?	☐ (10 points)	☐ (0 points)

(If there is a variety of plants, pests and disease are less likely to invade the area.)

Does your area include flowering plants? ☐ (10 points) ☐ (0 points)
(Flowering plants attract helpful and beautiful pollinators.)

Can you distinguish harmful insects and other creatures ☐ (10 points) ☐ (0 points)
from beneficial ones?
(Knowing the difference between those creatures that help us and those that cause damage keeps people from destroying helpful ones!)

Can you name two of each? Name them.

_____ Beneficial (2 points) _____ Beneficial (2 points)

_____ Harmful (2 points) _____ Harmful (2 points)

Do you maintain a compost bin? ☐ (10 points) ☐ (0 points)
(A person who composts is recycling, and that's a good thing!)

When do you water your plants or lawn?

☐ early morning (10 points)   ☐ midday (0 points)

☐ evening (5 points)   ☐ any time of day (0 points)
(It is best to water early in the morning so that little water is lost to evaporation.)

Do you keep your yard area clear of dead plants and litter? ☐ (10 points) ☐ (0 points)
(Dead and dying plants attract pests and diseases; litter is unattractive.)

Do you apply pesticide? ☐ (0 points) ☐ (10 points)

If you apply pesticide, when?

☐ early morning (0 points)   ☐ afternoon (5 points)

☐ evening (5 points)   ☐ any time of day (0 points)
(Applying pesticide in the morning may harm helpful pollinators.)

Do you use mulch around your plants? ☐ (10 points) ☐ (0 points)
(Mulch helps soil keep its moisture, discourages weeds and keeps soil from being compacted.)

Does your area contain any native plants? ☐ (10 points) ☐ (0 points)
(Native plants are those that typically grow in an area naturally. They need less water and care.)

When you use chemicals, how carefully do you follow the label's directions?

☐ Very carefully (10 points)   ☐ Use more chemical if it is a big problem. (0 points)
(When people use a chemical contrary to what the label recommends, it could be dangerous and pollute the environment.)

Score

(If the score is 90 points or more, this person is a Backyard Buddy!)

7

Backyard Buddy Award

presented to

_____

by the

Junior Master Gardener® Program

for using environmentally friendly practices in your community
and making the world a more beautiful place

_____
Junior Master Gardener®

_____
JMG® Leader

_____
JMG® Group Name

_____
Date

Life Skills and Career Exploration

I WANT YOU FOR JMG

NEAREST GARDEN

Teaching Concept 8

Activity 37:
Plant a Seed

Objective: Demonstrate the importance of being clear and concise when communicating

Time: 15-25 minutes

Materials: Container, potting soil, seeds, watering can and water

Explain to the students that it is very important to have good communication skills. It is important to be able to speak clearly with concise language so that other people understand us. We should think about what we are going to say and how we are going to say it before we actually speak it. If we are trying to explain something to someone, we should be as clear as we can. It is also important that we listen well to hear what others have to say.

This activity is an exercise in *both* speaking and listening. The most effective way to conduct this activity is to use two volunteers. Bring the two students to the front of the room and have them sit back to back so that they cannot see what the other is doing. Tell the students that one of them is going to be the "instruction giver" and the other is going to be the "doer." Tell them that they are going to be planting some seeds. The "doer" must follow the instruction giver's directions

exactly. For example, if the instruction giver says "put a seed in the pot," the "doer" should get the seed out of the package any way she chooses and put it in the pot with no soil.

Give the doer the following items: a small pot, a bag of soil, some seeds, and a container of water. Tell the students to begin and let the class watch how the seed is planted.

This activity can be comical because students often gloss over the specifics when giving instructions. When the "instruction giver" finally sees the end result of those brief instructions, the student is usually shocked that it hardly resembles a planted seed! After they have finished, follow up with some questions about the success or failure of the task. Was the seed planted correctly? Were there any steps that were out of order? Do you think this seed will germinate and grow? Then follow up with more

150

questions on communication skills. What could we have done to make the instructions more clear? Is it important that we listen to instructions? What kinds of instructions should we pay special attention to? What are some good ways to give clear instructions?

In the Classroom

Have the students complete the same activity by writing a "how to" paper on how to plant a seed. Have the students complete a draft of the steps to planting a seed and then ask for one volunteer to read her instructions as a "doer" follows them. After the class watches the first attempt to plant the seed, allow them time to revise or add to their instructions.

8

Activity 38:
Don't Label Me

Objective: Identify the positive traits of being a good friend and how labeling people can be hurtful

Time: 30 minutes

Materials: *Label Me* cards (page153), paper and pencils

Divide the students into groups of five or six and have them sit in a circle. Tape a *Label Me* card on the forehead of each student without allowing the students to see the label on their own cards. Explain to each student that they must remain quiet until all people have their labels and are ready to begin the activity. Be sure that each group has a variety of cards represented.

Tell the students that you are going to give them an assignment. As they work together to complete their assignment, they should treat the others in the group as the labels suggest.

Give each group a task to complete such as planning a class party or preparing to work on an area of the garden (such as watering or weeding).

Set a time limit for the students to complete the task and then have them begin discussions. Once the time limit has elapsed, talk about the activity and ask them if they can guess their label. Were they able to complete the task? Did the labeling get in the way of being able to work together? How did their label make them feel? Ask students if they think that labeling people is a good thing. Name some ways that people are hurtfully labeled. (For example, judging people by where they live, the color of their skin, the clothes they wear, or the language they speak.)

Have the students brainstorm about things they can do to make everyone feel welcome in their classes, schools and communities.

Label Me cards

Agree with me

Laugh at me

Make me do all the work

Ignore me

Disagree with me

Encourage me

Activity 39:
You're Great!

Objective: Learn the importance of giving people recognition and compliments

Time: 30 minutes

Materials: Paper, crayons or markers

Ask your JMGers if they like it when they are praised for something they have done. Tell your group that everyone enjoys being complimented. Point out to the group that their words and actions are powerful. Ask them to share their thoughts of how giving positive or negative words to another person makes the other people feel. Ask them if they feel it is important for others to feel good about themselves. Ask the group if they think feeling good about themselves affects the way they act.

Challenge them to always look for and pay attention to good qualities in others.

Provide a hat or bowl with a list of names of all of the students in the group. Each name should be in the hat four times. Have students draw four names. They should redraw if they draw the same name or their own name. When all names have been drawn, they should have the names of four different students.

They should then anonymously watch the four other people and look for a compliment to give that person. For example, one person may be good at cheering people up, another may be good with math, and another may be a good friend. Ask everyone to design a greeting

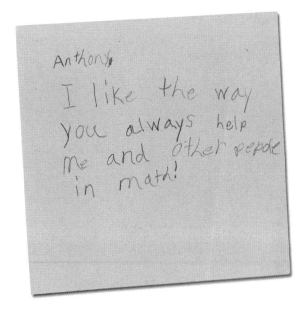

Anthony
I like the way you always help me and other pepole in math!

card or note, using paper, crayons, etc., to recognize a great quality or effort they noticed. They should do this for each of their four people.

Have the JMGers return the completed notes or cards to you labeled with the recipient's name. The next day, before the students arrive, place the compliments on the student's desk. Watch everyone's faces brighten as they come in and read their cards. Ask them how receiving positive messages makes them feel. Point out that they should all make it a habit to recognize the good efforts of those around them.

Activity 40:
Right on Target

Objective: Identify a personal goal and identify steps for achieving the goal

Time: 20 minutes

Materials: *My Targets for This Week* Worksheet

Distribute the My Targets for This Week worksheet to the students. Have everyone write in the center of the target one goal he or she is going to aim for during the week. Have them write in the outer rings the steps that they need to take to achieve their goal. It would be helpful to give an example so the group can see the process of goal-setting. See the example below.

At the end of the week, ask the group how many were able to hit their target and achieve at least one of their goals. Have them color each step of the target as they completed that step toward their goal. When a goal is reached, the entire bull's eye gets colored. Allow the students to share with the group the goal that they achieved.

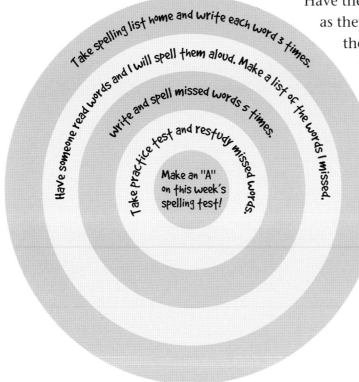

Take spelling list home and write each word 3 times.

Have someone read words and I will spell them aloud. Make a list of the words I missed.

Write and spell missed words 5 times.

Take practice test and restudy missed words.

Make an "A" on this week's spelling test!

In the Classroom

Have the students make a large bull's eye to post in the classroom. Help the students identify a goal that they would like to achieve as a group. The goal could be achieving a reading goal, improving test scores, finishing a leadership project, etc. Put that goal in the middle of the bull's eye. Encourage the students to identify the things that the class needs to do to achieve the goal. Have the students identify things individually that each of them have to do to reach the group goal.

8

My Targets for This Week

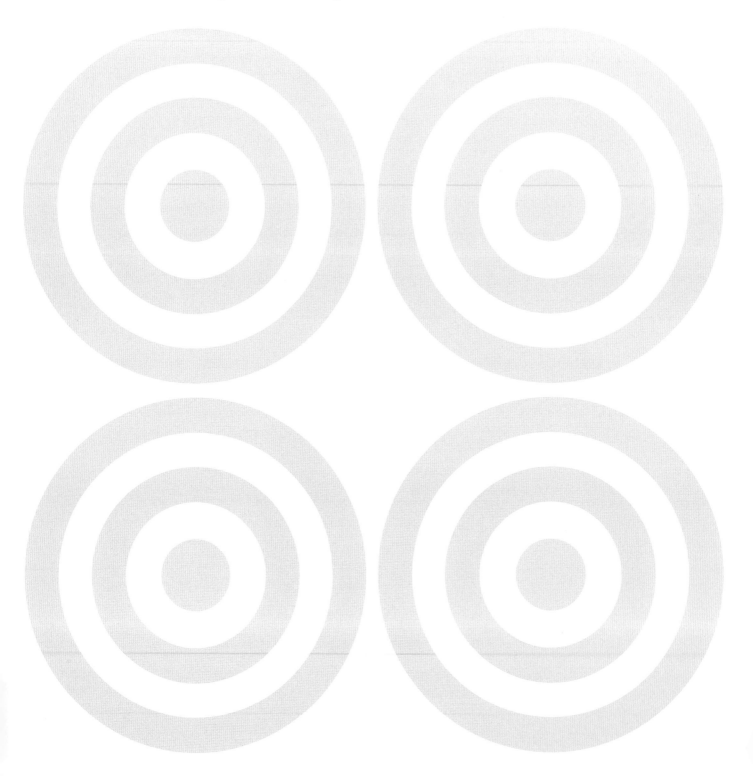

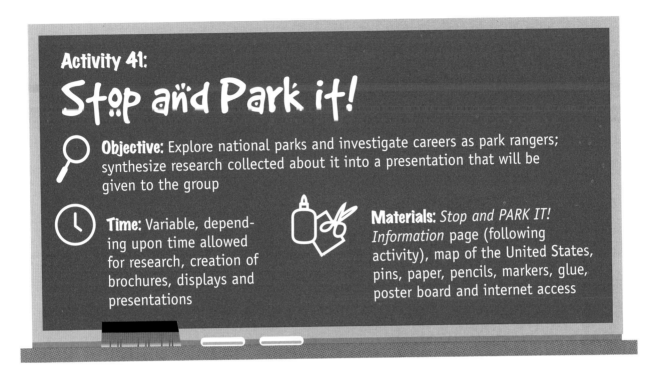

Activity 41:
Stop and Park it!

Objective: Explore national parks and investigate careers as park rangers; synthesize research collected about it into a presentation that will be given to the group

Time: Variable, depending upon time allowed for research, creation of brochures, displays and presentations

Materials: *Stop and PARK IT! Information* page (following activity), map of the United States, pins, paper, pencils, markers, glue, poster board and internet access

The purpose of this activity is to introduce students to many of the national parks in the United States. Visit resource links at *www.jmgkids.org/wildlifegardener* to access the National Parks Service sites and to identify national parks that might be of interest to the class. Use a map to mark these parks with pins labeled with the park name.

Ask the group to tell about the kinds of jobs adults have. Have the group describe the kind of work their parents do and the day-to-day tasks that make up those jobs. Ask students to share their ideas of their own future career possibilities. Tell your Wildlife Gardeners to imagine a job where they spend a lot of their day outdoors. This job could be in a very large and beautiful forest. Explain that the job is to care for and protect the forest or campgrounds and teach others about the forest. Explain that this describes some of

the jobs Park Rangers do when they go to work.

Divide the class into teams of 2-4 and explain to each team that they will be serving as Junior Park Rangers for a national park. Explain that national parks are special, usually very large places located around the country. Tell the group that Park Rangers are there to protect and preserve the park. Show each Park Ranger team the national park they are assigned to. As a team, their job is to represent their park to the entire class. Each team will be asked to create the following:

- A brochure, display board or booth for their park

- A presentation that encourages others to come and visit their park

To complete this assignment, team members first need to find information

8

about their park. Handout a copy of the Stop and PARK IT! Information page for each team member. Reiterate that one role of a park ranger is to educate visitors about the park. Students should become very familiar with the features of their assigned park so that they can share it with others. Students can use reference materials or visit resource links at *www.jmgkids.org/wildlifegardener* to complete their information pages.

Once the groups have researched their parks, allow them time to work to plan and complete a brochure and display that provides an overview for their park. If possible make sample brochures available to give teams ideas of how to combine images and text within their brochure. An easy form for the brochure to take would be in a front and back tri-fold brochure as shown below. Display boards containing the same information could also be created and include "sample materials" from the park.

If possible, hold a National Park Conference and allow other classes or groups of people to come and hear the team presentations and view the brochures and displays. Other classes could be given park passes and would get their passes stamped as they viewed each team presentation and display!

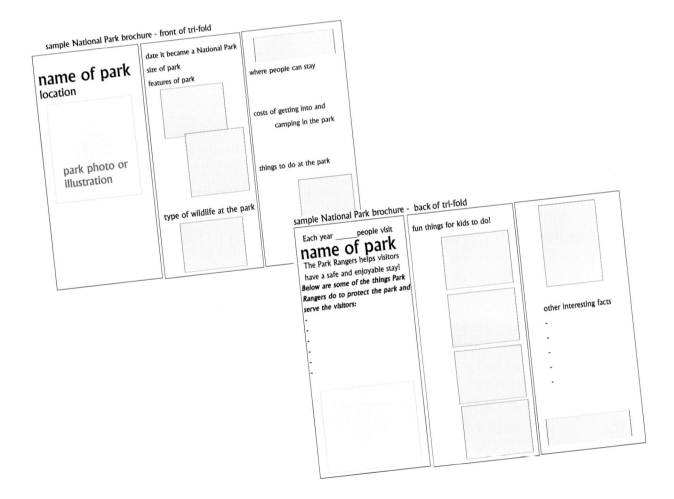

In the Classroom

When students locate information about their park total annual visitation, have students calculate the average number of visitors per day. Have students poll the class or school during the Park Conference on which attractions in their park would be of most interest. Determine if there is a correlation with points of greatest interest from the conference and the most widely visited parks.

Stop & PARK IT! Information

Name: _____

Where is the park located?_____

How old is the park? _____

How big is the park? _____

What are some of the most popular areas of the park?

_____

_____

What types of animals can you see at the park?

_____

_____

Where can you stay at the park?

_____

_____

How much does it cost to enter the park?

_____

_____

How many visitors go to the park each year?_____

What kind of programs or projects do they have for kids?

_____

_____

What is the role of the park rangers at the park?

_____

_____

What other interesting facts did you discover?

_____

_____

Service-Learning and Leadership Development Projects

The best way to culminate your JMG group's learning is through a worthwhile and gratifying service-learning project. A service project is also one requirement for youths to earn a certification as a Wildlife Gardener. Below are two service-learning and leadership development options for your group.

I. Establish a site as a NWF® Certified Schoolyard Habitat®.

Your group has likely already completed or will be completing many activities to establish components of habitat at your site. Once your group has implemented those components of wildlife habitat, complete the Schoolyard Habitat Application on pages 219-226. The application will help you document components of habitat you are implementing as well as how the area is/will be maintained and utilized. Applications are reviewed by the Schoolyard Habitats staff at the National Wildlife Federation to see if the basic criteria are met.

When your habitat is certified:

❀ You will be sent a Certificate of Achievement from the National Wildlife Federation.

❀ Your habitat will be assigned its own unique number and it will be entered in our computer-based National Registry of Schoolyard Habitats Sites.

❀ You will also receive the quarterly Habitats newsletter and information about how to stay active in the program.

❀ An announcement about your achievement will be sent by NWF to your local news media. This national recognition will help your efforts to raise funds in the future.

❀ You will also be able to join an online discussion group of Schoolyard Habitats practitioners, access NWF resources, information and expertise, and join a dynamic network of educators nationwide.

2. Create you own service-learning project!

Your group can create a service-learning project that incorporates what your group has learned through their Wildlife Gardener experiences! Involve your Wildlife Gardeners in helping to identify what particular needs might exist in your community then decide on a project, plan how it will be accomplished and implement the plan.

A

JMG® Registration Packet

The forms described below will be used in accounting, in tracking youths and leaders in the Junior Master Gardener program, and for ordering completion certificates.

1. JMG Registration Agreement Form

The JMG Registration Agreement Form registers a properly organized and functional JMG group. The registration serves as a permit for use of the 4-H and JMG service marks, names, logos and emblems. It allows a group to function with all the rights and privileges of 4-H/JMG membership.

2. JMG Member Group Enrollment Form (JMG 1-5.061)

The JMG program reaches hundreds of thousands of youths across the nation. To document each youth's participation in the program, the teacher and/or leader must complete form JMG 1-5.061 for each group. JMG 1-5.061 will provide statistical data for state and federal governments for future funding and civil rights documentation.

Use these guidelines when completing the JMG Junior Master Gardener Member Group Enrollment Form:

County Name: County in which the JMG program is being conducted

JMG Group Name: This name can be created by the youths (something catchy, or related to region)

JMG Group Teacher/Leader: Name of classroom teacher and/or leader (A registration form must be included for each teacher/leader named.)

SECTION I: Unit Information
The JMG program can be organized in several ways:

Community: A community 4-H club having club officers, regular monthly meetings, a community service project, project meetings, a club manager, parental participation and project leaders.

Project: Same as a community club, except that it concentrates on only one project and expands into other projects after the original one.

School: Same as community club, except that it is organized and conducted in school; members may be divided into several clubs of different ages.

Curriculum Enrichment:	A learning activity in a classroom setting, led by teacher, a staff member or a volunteer. The project consists of at least six learning experiences, each 20 to 60 minutes long.
Community Partnership:	Has the same structure as a community club and can be delivered in a school setting. However, the lead volunteers managing the club come from at least two other distinct organizations whose goal or project is to work with youths (e.g., Lions Club, Key Club, etc.).
Special Interest:	Organized or coordinated by Extension personnel and directed and/or taught by volunteer adult or youth leaders. The meetings are conducted in informal classroom settings with members participating in at least 20- to 60-minute learning sessions with the total learning time of at least 2 hours.
Camping:	Youth program in a structured, informal setting ranging from 1 full day to overnight.
ENP-Y:	(Expanded Nutrition Program - Youth). Program designed to teach good nutrition and health. This program involves youth in all aspects of food production and consumption and can be delivered at schools as curriculum enrichment, in after-school programs or neighborhood groups, at recreation centers and summer day camps, and/or as displays at community health fairs.
Clover Kids (K-2):	Informal educational program for youths ages 5 to 8 in kindergarten, first and second grades. This program is an introductory 4-H program for boys and girls.

SECTION II - Distribution of Member by:

Record information in this section as accurately as possible. Make sure that each person in the project is accounted for and that the totals in all four boxes match. If the RACE AND GENDER Section reflects that all participants are of the same race, then please complete the two questions under the box. This will provide civil rights documentation concerning the setting of the project and its accessibility to all races and sexes.

3. JMG Junior Master Gardener Leader/ Teacher Registration Form (JMG 2-1.056)

All teachers and volunteers must complete this form, which will be used to gather statistical information on all volunteers and teachers in the program. The back of the registration form is an optional volunteer screening process. After completing these forms, schoolteachers and officials are strongly encouraged to review the information about all volunteers before beginning the program.

The teachers and/or volunteer leaders should complete this form at the beginning of each new class of Junior Master Gardeners.

4. JMG Completion Form

Once your group has completed certification requirements (page XVII), mail the completed JMG Completion Order Form to the Junior Master Gardener headquarters.

Mail all forms to:

Junior Master Gardener
Headquarters
225 HFSB
Texas A&M University, M.S. 2134
College Station, Texas 77843-2134
(979) 845-8565
FAX (979) 845-8906
E-mail: programinfo@jmgkids.org

You will receive from the JMG Program headquarters an official letter of registration for your group. A copy of your Registration Packet will be sent to your local or state Extension office for its records.

When members of your group complete the JMG curriculum requirements, order JMG Certificates by completing the JMG Completion Form and mailing it to the JMG Program headquarters at Texas A&M University. Certificates will be returned promptly so you can present them to the newest Junior Master Gardeners!

JMG® Junior Master Gardener® Registration Agreement Form

**We request through this Registration Agreement Form to be an official JMG group.
Our group has met all of the following criteria:**
1. A minimum of five youths
2. One or more adult teacher/leader(s)
3. Suitable meeting facilities (classroom, garden area)
4. An official club or group name (JMG office reserves the right to modify name)

JMG group name desired _____

JMG site/campus/district _____

County where JMG group is located _____

Designated JMG Teacher/Leader _____   Date _____

    Address   _____   Telephone _____

       _____   e-mail _____
            City   State   ZIP
           (Notify of any address changes)

Submitting this form:
The group teacher/leader should complete this form and submit it to the JMG Program headquarters at Texas A&M University:

       Junior Master Gardener Program
       225 Horticulture/Forestry Science Building
       Texas A&M University
       College Station, Texas 77843-2134
       Phone: (979) 845-8565
       Fax: (979) 845-8906

If you have questions about registering, or need help with the registration forms, please call us!

Educational programs conducted by Texas Cooperative Extension serve people of all ages regardless of socioeconomic level, race, color, sex, religion, disability, or national origin.

Check:

❏ I have read the JMG Management Guide and agree to follow the JMG guidelines.

❏ I agree to assist in protecting the service marks and copyright of the JMG program as described.

_____
JMG Teacher/Leader signature   Date

Form 1 of 4

A

JMG® Junior Master Gardener® Member Group Enrollment Form JMG 1-5.061

Date _____ / _____ / _____

County Name _____
JMG Group Name _____
JMG Group Teacher/Leader _____

SECTION I - Unit Information: Type of 4-H organization (Check only one)

- ☐ 1. Community
- ☐ 2. Project
- ☐ 3. School
- ☐ 4. Community Partnership
- ☐ 5. Special Interest
- ☐ 6. Curriculum Enrichment
- ☐ 7. Camping
- ☐ 8. ENP-Y
- ☐ 9. Clover Kids (K-2)

SECTION II - Distribution of Members by:
Totals in this section for age, residence and race and gender should all be the same.

AGE

Age	Number
Under 9	
9	
10	
11	
12	
13	
14	
15	
16	
17	
18	
19	

RESIDENCE

Residence	Number
Rural/Farm	
Town less than 10,000	
City between 10,000 and 50,000	
Suburb of city more than 50,000	
Central city more than 50,000	
Total	

JMG PROJECT CODE

Code	10089
Males	
Females	

RACE AND GENDER

	Males	Females	Totals
White - not of Hispanic origin			
Black - not of Hispanic origin			
American Indian or Alaskan Native			
Hispanic			
Asian or Pacific Islander			
Totals			

If all participants are of the same race, please answer the following questions:

Is this unit in a racially mixed community (at least two different racial groups)? ☐ Yes ☐ No

Is this unit integrated? ☐ Yes ☐ No

JMG® Junior Master Gardener® Leader/Teacher Registration Form JMG 2-1.065

JMG Group Name _____   Unit/Club Number _____

Check (✓) preference   ❏ Mr.   ❏ Mrs.   ❏ Ms.   ❏ Dr.

Name _____

(Last)   (First)   (Middle Initial)

Mailing Address _____

City/Town _____   Zip Code _____

Phone Number: Home (___)_____   Work (___)_____

E-mail Address: _____   ❏ Male   ❏ Female   ❏ Adult   ❏ Youth

This information is requested to gather statistics for compliance with nondiscrimination requirements.

Check (✓) only one
❏ 1. American Indian or Alaskan Native
❏ 2. Asian or Pacific Islander
❏ 3. Black - not Hispanic origin
❏ 4. Hispanic
❏ 5. White - not of Hispanic origin

Code	Project Name
10089	Junior Master Gardener

Years as a 4-H Leader (including this year) _____

Residence

Check (✓) only one
❏ 1. Rural/Farm
❏ 2. Town less than 10,000
❏ 3. City between 10,000 and 50,000
❏ 4. Suburb of city more than 50,000
❏ 5. Central city more than 50,000

Major Leadership Responsibility
❏ 1. Club Manager
❏ 2. Project Leader
❏ 3. Activity Leader
❏ 4. JMG Volunteer (specify)
_____
❏ 5. Other (teacher, etc.)
_____

4-H Alumni: ❏ Yes   ❏ No

State _____
County _____

Do you work directly with youth?
❏ Yes   ❏ No

Type of 4-H Unit

Check (✓) only one
❏ 1. Community
❏ 2. Project
❏ 3. School
❏ 4. Community Partnership
❏ 5. Clover Kids (K-2)
❏ 6. Special Interest
❏ 7. Curriculum Enrichment
❏ 8. Camping
❏ 9. ENP-Y

_____   _____
Date   Signature

Form 3 of 4

A

173

 **Appendix**

The following information is requested in support of the Texas 4-H JMG Program's commitment to continually guarantee the safety of the members during 4-H participation.

Volunteer Interest *(To be completed by volunteers 18 years or older)*
Have you previously served as a 4-H volunteer?   ☐ Yes   ☐ No
If yes, where? _____ County _____ State _____
And how many years? _____

Personal Information
Do you have a current/valid driver's license?   ☐ Yes   ☐ No   If Yes, Driver's License # _____
Do you have automobile liability insurance?   ☐ Yes   ☐ No

Have you ever been convicted of a violation of any local, state or federal law, **other than minor traffic violations?** (This includes a plea of guilty or no contest.)   ☐ Yes   ☐ No   **If YES,** list all convictions below, from the oldest to the most recent.

Date of Conviction Month and Year	Mark appropriate box		Offense (Do not use abbreviations)
	Misdemeanor	Felony	

References

1. Name _____
   Address _____
   City _____ Zip _____
   Telephone _____

2. Name _____
   Address _____
   City _____ Zip _____
   Telephone _____

3. Name _____
   Address _____
   City _____ Zip _____
   Telephone _____

I certify that the statements made by me on this registration form are true, complete and correct to the best of my knowledge and belief and are made in good faith. I understand that any false statement made herein will void this registration form and any actions based upon it. I authorize the 4-H JMG Program or any of its components to make reference checks relating to my volunteer service. I understand that this application and all attachments are the property of the Texas 4-H & Youth Development Program.

_____   _____
Date   Volunteer Signature

Form 4 of 4

JMG® Junior Master Gardener® Completion Form

(For Certificates - Duplicate as Needed)

Upon completion of the JMG curriculum requirements, fill out this form to request JMG Certificates for your group members. Mail the completed form to Junior Master Gardener Program, 225 HFSB, Texas A&M University, College Station, Texas 77843-2134.

Date: _____ County: _____ JMG Group Name: _____

| NAME | PROGRAM COMPLETED | | UNIT(S) COMPLETED (ie – Wildlife Gardener, Ch. 2, Soils and Water, etc.) | Estimate the total number of hours of service your group performed.* |
	JMG	GOLDEN RAY SERIES		

_____ total hours of service

I certify that these JMG group members have completed all of the requirements to receive certification.

Teacher/Leader Name: _____ Signature: _____ Date: _____

Certificates should be mailed to the following address: _____

Phone (____) _____ City _____ State _____ Zip _____

* This is just a rough estimate of the number of hours your group worked to complete your service project(s) multiplied by the number of youths in taking part in the effort. For example, if your class spent about 6 total hours working on a project and there are 20 students in your group, that would be a total of 120 hours of service contributed by your group!

A

A

Garden Preparation and Planting Instructions

Getting Started

This section discusses the basic steps in establishing a garden habitat setting, as well as more specific tips on gardening with children through JMG youth gardening projects. This information can be used as a handy reference guide with any of the JMG garden projects or units. Keep them handy as you plan your program!

We encourage you to involve your JMG group as much as possible in the development process of your group's wildlife garden. By allowing them to participate in selecting the site and deciding what to grow, you will be empowering your students while developing leadership and teamwork skills, which are an essential part of the JMG program.

Garden Planning and Preparation

Site Selection: What location will be best?
(See Activity 1: P.L.A.N.T. and Wildlife Needs, page 2)

Take some time to think through the following factors before deciding on a location for your garden.

The site should have:

Easy access
Locate it as close as possible to the building where your group meets. The easier it is to access, the more convenient it is for you and your JMGers to use, and the more use you will get out of it. A closer location also usually results in better maintenance and a lower potential for vandalism, and makes those inevitable trips back inside for forgotten supplies or for bathroom breaks easier to manage.

A Location Offering Sunny and Shady Areas
Different plants and various forms of wildlife thrive in very different conditions. A location that offers both sunny and shady areas will provide for these diverse needs. Most wildlife will benefit from the different food and shelters offered by a variety of full sun to full shade plants. Remember, gardens including vegetables will require 6-8 hours of full sun each day. In addition a host of shade plants that can complement your garden habitat. Most wildlife will seek the coolness that shade provides. A shady spot near the garden is also great for rest breaks. Partial shade from trees or nearby buildings can help serve that purpose.

Nearby Water Source

Water is critical to the sustainability of your garden habitat area. Your group will need access to water for watering the garden, replenishing water sources as well as for tool (and child) cleanup. Lugging water hoses across a field is inconvenient and difficult. If there is a maintenance person in charge of the water from whom you will need to get a key each time you need water, make friends with them early on in the process!

Loose, Well-Drained Soil

Depending on the plants and wildlife your will be working to include in your garden habitat, you will want to consider the soil at the site. Locate the garden in a spot where water drains well after rain. Constantly wet or waterlogged soil will drown plant roots. Well dug, raised beds enclosed by landscape timbers, or other edging will greatly improve water drainage and air movement in soil.

In general, think through the potential site from all possible angles. Make it as easy and convenient as possible on both yourself and your JMG group. You want your group to spend your time learning about and enjoying your garden—not wasting time carrying supplies and getting less enjoyment from the experience because it is inconvenient or difficult to manage.

Planting Guidelines

There are two basic methods of planting: direct seeding, and transplanting. Many garden habitats can benefit from a combination of both methods.

> Remember that native plants are those that could naturally occur in a given area. Native plants thrive in their natural environment and naturally offer components of habitat to native wildlife. As you are thinking about plants to add to your garden habitat, findout more about native plants and native plant resources in your state by contacting your local county Extension office, plant nursery or by visiting links at: www.jmgkids.org/wildlifegardener

Direct seeding

- Direct seeding is simply planting seeds directly into the garden.

- Direct seeding offers several advantages over transplanting. A packet of seeds is usually cheaper than a pack of transplants and you get many more potential plants in a packet of seeds.

- Some plants, such as wildflowers are best planted from seed because transplanting disturbs their roots and may stunt their growth.

- Seeds can be purchased from your local nursery or garden center, or can be requested from seed company catalogs. Looking through seed catalogs and making a wish list is a fun project for adults and kids alike and will give your JMG group practice in garden planning and design.

A

- Seed companies may offer catalogs free of charge and many are willing to send you multiple copies for your group to use in garden planning projects. If you let them know you are working with a JMG youth gardening program many will donate seeds or allow you to purchase at a discount. Plant people are great!

- Follow planting directions on the seed packet carefully! The most common mistakes when planting seeds are planting them too deep or washing them away when watering. When planting seeds, a general rule of thumb is to plant them twice as deep as they are wide. However, some seeds have special requirements with regard to planting depth—check the packet!

- Newly planted seeds must be kept moist until they germinate and form their own root systems capable of absorbing water in the soil. Use a very gentle spray to avoid washing seeds out of their row. Watering wands work great for children and the garden.

Transplanting

- Transplanting is planting small plants in your garden which are already growing, such as multi-packs or small pots of plants purchased from a nursery or seedlings that your JMG group raised indoors.

- Some plants take a long time to grow and establish themselves, so are usually sown indoors ahead of time and transplanted out to the garden as already-growing plants at the appropriate time. Examples are tomatoes and peppers.

- Still other plants are difficult to grow from seed at all and may require special conditions or long periods of time to germinate and are best grown from transplants.

- Transplanting is more expensive per plant than direct seeding but most crops grown this way require less time, space and seed or seedling.

- Starting seeds indoors is an excellent project. The main ingredient needed for most healthy seedlings is a lot of light—bright indirect light from a window or artificial light from a purchased unit. Without adequate light seedlings will be spindly and unhealthy, and will not perform well in the garden.

Garden Maintenance
Watering
Newly seeded or planted areas need to be checked daily and kept moist until the small plants establish root systems allowing roots to absorb moisture from surrounding soil. Seedlings get their water from the immediate rootzone area. Once plants are established, usually after 1-2 weeks, they will need longer but less frequent watering. It is better to water two to three times a week than to sprinkle lightly every day. This encourages roots to penetrate deeper into the soil.

All plants do not use and need water at the same rate. Some are more drought tolerant than others. Show your group how to check whether their plants need water. If they stick their finger into the top inch of the soil (about to their first knuckle) and it is dry, then water. If it is damp under the surface, it doesn't need water. Signs of wilting may mean plants need water. Wilting can also be a sign of over watering, thus the importance of finger checking.

Native plants are more likely to rely on naturally occurring growing conditions than others.

Watch out for the water hose! Strong blasts of water can uproot and wash away plants. You can make watering cans out of plastic one quart milk jugs with holes punched in the lids. This allows each gardener to have a controlled amount of water to irrigate the garden. The jugs can easily be refilled if more is needed and each child gets to water their own plants.

Fertilizing

A few plants your group installs in a garden area may require periodic fertilization. If needed, a very easy way to fertilize is to use a water-soluble fertilizer. It can be easily spooned into jugs as students fill them, and the plants will get fertilized as they are being hand watered.

Make sure to read the label carefully so that you know what you are getting, and apply the correct amount according to directions. In the case of plant fertilizer, *less is best*. More fertilizer does not equal more plant growth. If plants get too much fertilizer, or if concentrated fertilizer is left on plant leaves, the plants may experience fertilizer burn and die.

Weeding

A weed is just an unwanted plant. Removing weeds will be more important to some groups than others. The good thing about weeding is that it goes quickly when done regularly and it encourages close observation. Make it a part of your weekly routine—afterwards observations can be written into journals.

Pest

Inspection will need to be done periodically. If you have a garden with a lot of different varieties of plants, you will probably not have too many pest outbreaks. When multiple smaller crops are produced, large numbers of pests do not usually build up as they do when large areas of one crop, called a monoculture, are produced. Monocultures allow large numbers of pest populations to build up. Maintaining healthy plants will also lessen pest damage; weak, malnourished or weed-ridden plants are more prone to attract pests. Still, the most diversified, well-maintained garden will have an occasional pest outbreak. Having a plan developed in advance will enable you to act quickly to minimize damage. The Junior Master Gardener Program

181

A

recommends IPM—Integrated Pest Management—as a pest management strategy. (See Activity 26: Who Goes There?, page 98)

Check with your officials to find out what other regulations there are and follow them! There may be a designated person for pesticide applications or restrictions as to when they can be applied. Also, rules for schools or private businesses may be different than those for homeowners.

Tools and Equipment

- There is no set list of required tools and equipment for children's gardens. Review these suggestions and develop a list that will best fit your needs.

- Tools can be borrowed for volunteer work days when you will have larger than normal groups of adults working; however, one or two shovels, rakes, and hoes are good to have on hand for ongoing maintenance needs.

- Inexpensive child-sized shovels, rakes, and hoes are now available and can be found at many hardware stores or garden centers. These are great for kids because they are not play tools. They have wooden handles and metal heads just like standard-sized tools, but are proportioned smaller for children. You can also adapt standard-sized tools that are donated by cutting off handles.

- Garden bed preparation, especially with raised beds, will require shovels and rakes for mixing and spreading soil. However, once the garden is established, children can do almost

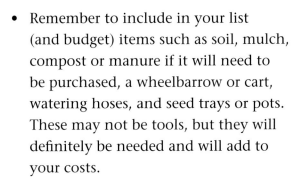

everything they will need to do with hand tools. These are less expensive to purchase and replace if lost or broken, and present less safety hazards for use with groups of children.

- Make sure to go over safety rules with your group.

- Remember to include in your list (and budget) items such as soil, mulch, compost or manure if it will need to be purchased, a wheelbarrow or cart, watering hoses, and seed trays or pots. These may not be tools, but they will definitely be needed and will add to your costs.

- Make a list and then go through it to determine which items you can use coupons or have donated before purchasing.

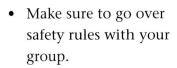
Garden Management Tips for Group Leaders

Managing Students

While big groups can work larger areas of garden space, smaller groups of 5 or less students each are more successful and easier to manage. Dividing large groups into smaller ones allows for more ownership of garden plots, and provides opportunities for exploration, observation, as well as for individual responsibilities within projects.

Young gardeners are naturally active so plan for them to stay busy in the garden habitat area. Having gardeners sit while waiting for their turn to work in the garden will likely lead them to be distracted and board. Either pull groups of students away from a larger group activity to work in the garden or give each of the groups specific tasks to complete.

While one small group is weeding, another group could be measuring growth and another watering the plants of their individual gardens. Also, it is a good idea to have another assignment waiting for when their task is completed. This second task will serve as a time buffer for the groups that finish early or at different times. For example, as groups finish their jobs, they might have the responsibility of writing in the journals, clearing an area of litter, writing thank you notes to helpers, sketching from the garden, taking leaf rubbings or relaxing with a book.

Another successful method is to have gardeners rotate through different tasks so that each group can experience all activities as a small group. Volunteers can be a way to aid in managing small groups and giving gardeners individual attention.

Getting Help: Recruiting Volunteers

Don't be hesitant to ask for volunteer help with garden projects. Work days

that include youths as well as parents, grandparents, Master Gardeners, and local professionals can accomplish a great deal and establish a shared ownership of the garden.

In addition to scheduled workdays, you will probably need to get some outside help from other adults for recruiting donations and other garden coordination activities. Establishing a JMG Garden Committee will enable you to keep all those involved updated on garden plans and developments, and helps spread out some of the duties involved in coordinating a JMG garden program. Your JMG Committee can include administrators, local business representatives, program co-workers and maintenance staff such as teachers and custodians, parent volunteers, and of course, student representatives from the JMG group.

Funding Your Garden

Gardening can be done by spending very little money, or can be a large expense, depending on the amount and type of structure and supplies that are used.

Some groups start with a small garden habitat area and will often develop into a larger setting. However, using the garden as a learning

environment is more important than funding an elaborate setup.

There are many ways to obtain the supplies and funds that you will need for your garden. Following are a few suggestions, but they are by no means the only options. Be creative!

- **Donations** of supplies, plants, and seeds are often easier to obtain than money with which to buy them. *Local nurseries* will often donate plants and/or seeds – especially if you are willing to utilize old seed or plants with minor damage. *Local landscapers* may donate topsoil, mulch, or landscape plantings for the garden, especially if they have children in your school or program. A *wish list* sent home with students can often generate donations of equipment such as an old wheelbarrow or cart, watering hoses and sprinklers, or pots and buckets to use as planting containers. Remember to thank donors by having gardeners write thank you letters, or by putting a sign in the garden thanking sponsors. This provides them with free advertising, and can help generate future donations.

- **Fundraisers** planned and coordinated by gardeners generate funds to purchase garden tools and other needed items, and also enables them to practice and develop business and leadership skills. Baked goods or other products can be conducted

to generate initial funds. If a vegetable or herb garden is established there are many garden products like fresh produce and herbal crafts, which can be sold. Many school garden programs establish accounts with funds from sales to pay for tools and equipment or to generate scholarships for students. You can do the same with your JMG group.

- **Grants** are available to fund hands-on education programs such as JMG youth gardens. There is a vast array of grants that you can apply for. These range from relatively small local community grants to larger private foundations as well as state and federally funded grant programs. Don't be afraid to pursue grant funds! Remember that local programs usually offer the best chance for success on an individual garden level. Check with your local garden clubs, garden centers, and community service agencies for potential programs. For additional information regarding sources of grants, visit: *www.jmgkids.org/grants*

- **Generating publicity** through the local newspaper and making contacts with local and regional community leaders are critical to promote awareness of your program and its benefits for local youths, along with an awareness of your group's needs. Local support—volunteer assistance and donations of equipment and funds—often results from such awareness. Phone calls and emails to local newspapers and television stations to make them aware of unique events such as a large garden work day, youths completing a service project, the certification of the garden habitat as a Schoolyard Habitat®, or a classroom of students earning their certification as Wildlife Gardenerssm.

Safety Considerations

Always remember to consider safety issues first in any project. Tool safety should be reviewed with gardeners. Also, know in advance of any allergies that your gardeners may have. Work with a school nurse and/or parents to develop a proactive safety plan in case of stings, bites, or exposures to plant allergies.

Vandalism

Vandalism is an unfortunate possibility that comes along with gardening in public spaces. In community gardens vandalism may be a result of older children in the same area or may be teenagers hanging out in the neighborhood after hours. Leaders who have gone through vandalism experiences with their students tend to regard it as an unfortunate fact of life that brings home some powerful lessons for young gardeners. However, they report that it is not a reason to not garden. Their advice: if it happens, make it a part of the learning experience. Note to gardeners that vandalism is a hurtful act and use the experience to initiate discussion on social responsibility, respect for self and others, and personal choices when dealing with peer pressure.

A

Planning a Garden Work Day

A

 **Appendix**

Planning a Garden Work Day

The garden can be a wonderful unifying place for people. However, in order to ensure that gardens are sustainable it is important that the garden be viewed as a community not an individual activity. Garden workdays can be a vital part of maintaining a garden area and offers a wonderful opportunity to solicit the involvement and ownership of others. Listed below are some tips for successful garden workdays.

1. Develop a garden committee that consists of the wide range of stakeholders that can be involved in the garden. As the committee is being formed, be sure to invite teachers/leaders, parents, administrators, local business people, Extension agents and children to join the effort. A garden committee can assist in establishing goals for the garden, uses of the garden, garden rules, garden maintenance plans, soliciting volunteers, seeking donations and writing grants.

2. When selecting garden workdays chose a variety of days of the week and weekend and times in order to allow for maximum participation. For example, if a garden workday is planned at 10:00am on a Saturday morning, you might be missing kids and families involved in soccer. Or a workday planned during the early evening of a weekday may preclude families that may be involved in church functions from attending.

3. Advertise the workday one to two weeks in advance then send a reminder four to five days before. Don't be shy about asking volunteers to bring along specific tools (such as rakes or shovels) or equipment(such as a tiller) if it is need. You might be surprised at the resources your volunteers have access to!

4. Keep garden workdays and meetings short and to the point. Be sure that you have a specific identified task, complete the task, and then adjourn. This will help facilitate future assistance. A garden workday of one to three hours is plenty!

5. If possible include refreshments for your meetings and workdays or be sure to remind your volunteers to bring their own.

6. Following the workday or meeting, encourage the children to write thank you notes to volunteers and others who participated – volunteers that know their efforts are appreciated are more likely to continue to volunteer.

7. Utilize the volunteer solicitation letter (page 190) as a way to bring other volunteers to assist with the garden effort. There are many ways to utilize volunteers based on their strengths, talents, and wishes. Finding out HOW people would like to participate in the project will ultimately make the project more successful.

A

Sample Volunteer solicitation letter

(DATE)

Dear Parents,

(Your School Name) is starting a Junior Master Gardener(JMG) program that will help our children grow and learn through a "hands-on" learning experiences and activities. The JMG program provides a positive learning experience for youth to develop leadership, responsibility and community pride through organized gardening activities. The JMG program combines a unique gardening based curriculum and web based instruction, community service, character education and service-based learning, into a fun and exciting certification program for youth. This program is designed to incorporate science, math, language arts, geography and other subject area disciplines into the "hands-on" gardening based activities. JMG curriculum is correlated to academic standards and has research supporting how the program improves academic success, nutrition, self-esteem, and leadership development. *(Your School Name)* needs your help to make the JMG program a success! Here are some ways you can become involved.

I am willing to:

_____ Serve on a *(Your School Name)* Junior Master Gardener Garden committee. This group will be made up of administrators, teacher, parents, and students.

_____ Assist in building garden beds, fences, arbors, and other structures.

_____ Donate money or gardening equipment and/or supplies for use in the garden.

_____ Volunteer my time to assist children in the garden or classroom.

_____ Assist by contacting businesses and community members for support through donations and gifts for the gardens.

Parent_____ **Child**_____

My child's teacher is _____.

Sample parent solicitation letter created by T. Ledbetter, teacher

Name _____ Date _____

Insect Templates

A

Name _____ Date _____

1 inch Grid Paper

Name _____ Date _____

1 Centimeter Grid Paper

A

Read the next 2 selections on frogs and toads. Then answer the questions that follow it.

Timothy's Report About Frogs

Timothy Davis
Grade 4
November 20, 2003

Interesting Facts About Frogs

1   Did you know that frogs use their eyeballs to help them eat? They push their eyes down into their heads to force the food down their throats. I couldn't believe my own ears when my science teacher told me that amazing fact! I decided that I wanted to learn more about frogs, so I visited my school library. It was there that I discovered even more interesting facts.

2   Frogs are amphibians. This means that they are cold-blooded animals with backbones. They are found on every continent except Antarctica. In the United States, there are 80 different species, or kinds, of frogs. The largest frog in the world is the foot long Goliath Frog in West Africa, and the smallest frog lives in Cuba. It is only 1/2 inch long!

3   No matter where frogs live in the world, they need to stay close to water. Their smooth skin must be kept *moist,* so they jump into ponds or lakes to stay wet. They even soak up water through their skin instead of drinking it. You should never hold a frog for too long, because if you do, its delicate skin will dry out quickly.

4   Because frogs swim in the water, their hind legs are long. Bullfrogs, the largest frogs in the United States, use their strong legs to leap great distances as they hunt for food near lakes and ponds. Like many other types of frogs, they have webbed hind feet to help them swim. Frogs have been known to jump up as far as twenty times the length of their bodies!

5   When frogs are babies, they can't jump at all. This is because they don't have legs. Female frogs lay clusters of eggs in water, and about 21 days later, tiny tadpoles hatch. Legs finally begin to sprout after about 6 weeks. The new frogs are able to leave their water homes after about 16 weeks.

6   After leaving the water, frogs will eat just about anything that fits into their mouths. They gulp down insects and spiders, and they have even been known to swallow mice and snakes. They use their long tongues to snap at their food. Then they close their bulging eyes and push their eyeballs down, forcing the food down their throats!

7   I think the most interesting thing about frogs is what they do when they eat things that make them feel bad. A frog will throw up its stomach so that it sticks out of its mouth! Next, it wipes its stomach clean by using its front leg. Finally, it swallows its newly-cleaned stomach.

8   Now that I know these cool facts about frogs, I think I want to learn about toads. I wonder if they do the same kinds of things as frogs!

Kiara's Report About Toads

Kiara Mason
Grade 4
November 20, 2003

Information About Toads

1   Last week my dog, Bingo, tried to eat a toad that he caught in our backyard. I was surprised when Bingo started pawing at his mouth, drooling and whimpering. Then I remembered that toads have poison glands behind their eyes. Bingo didn't get too sick from the poison, but I don't think he'll bother toads again! He learned about toads the hard way! Luckily, I learned about toads by researching the Internet. Toads are amphibians, and they have special traits, or qualities, that set them apart from true frogs.

2   First, toads have bumpy, warty skin. The bumps help them to blend in with their surroundings. Toad skin is also tough, so it doesn't dry out as fast as frog skin. Toads can live away from water, burrowing into the soil for moisture and protection from the sun. For example, the Texas Toad likes to live in grasslands and areas with sandy soil.

3   Second, since toads don't need to swim in water to protect their skin, their hind legs are short and they don't have webbed feet. They walk or make small hops on the ground to move around. They also use their claw-like fingers to dig into the soil.

4   Next, toads lay their eggs in long chains. Even though toads spend most of their lives out of water, they return to lakes and ponds to lay their eggs. After an average of 21 days, the eggs hatch. The tadpoles swim around and gradually develop into toads that can leave the water.

5   Finally, toads have short tongues that they use to snap up their meals. They will sneak up from behind and quickly grab their prey with their mouths. Toads gulp down insects and other animals that they can swallow whole.

6   Toads have been around for millions of years, so they have adapted well to their surroundings. Even so, they are sensitive animals, and we should be very careful when handling them. My dog certainly knows that now!

A

frog and Toad Questions

Use "Timothy's Report About Frogs" to answer questions 1-5.

1 Which word in paragraph 3 helps the reader to know what *moist* means?

A skin

B wet

C jump

D smooth

2 Paragraph 4 of the report is mainly about

A how frogs use their hind legs

B how frogs swim

C where frogs hunt for food

D types of frogs

3 What is the purpose of Timothy's report?

A To describe his experience of catching frogs

B To tell about different kinds of amphibians

C To persuade readers to buy frogs

D To inform readers about frog facts

4 Read the chart of events.

Frog's Early Life Cycle

* Females lay clusters of eggs.
* Tadpoles hatch.
* _____
* Frogs leave their water homes.

Which of the following best completes the chart?

A Tadpoles snap at their food

B Legs begin to sprout

C Tadpoles become babies

D Tadpoles leave their water homes

5 Which sentence from the report best shows that the author is interested in frogs?

A I wonder if they do the same kinds of things as frogs

B No matter where frogs live in the world, they need to stay close to water

C I decided that I wanted to learn more about frogs, so I visited my school library

D Frogs are amphibians

Use "Kiara's Report About Toads" to answer questions 6-9.

6 From the report, what can the reader tell about the Texas Toad?

A It lays its eggs in long chains

B It has webbed feet

C It has a long tongue

D It has smooth skin

7 In paragraph 1 of the report, the word traits means

A special

B toads

C amphibians

D qualities

8 Why don't toads dry out as quickly as frogs?

A They have webbed feet to swim in the water

B Their skin is tougher than frog skin

C They become tadpoles

D They use their poison glands

9 How does Kiara feel when she sees that her dog has been poisoned by a toad?

A She is surprised that Bingo ate the entire toad

B She feels lucky that she knows not to bother toads, unlike her dog

C She is angry at the toad for making her dog drool

D She is sad that the toad has poison glands

Use "Timothy's Report About Frogs" and "Kiara's Report About Toads" to answer questions 10-12.

10 Look at the chart below.

Frogs

* have smooth skin
* have long hind legs
* lay eggs in clusters

Toads
* have bumpy, warty skin
* have short hind legs
* _____

Which statement best completes the chart?

A walk or hop to move around

B must be kept moist

C hatch into tadpoles

D lay eggs in long chains

11 How are frogs and toads most alike?

A They jump as far as twenty times the length of their bodies.

B They are amphibians.

C They hunt for food near lakes and ponds.

D They have tough skin.

12 Timothy's report and Kiara's report both tell about how

A we should be careful when handling frogs or toads

B frogs or toads are large amphibians

C poison can hurt frogs and toads

D frogs are better than toads

A

197

Read this selection. Then answer the questions that follow it.

Mini-Meadow

Meadows are open, grassy areas that can support many kinds of wildlife. Meadow areas can be quite small, and it is even possible for people to create their own mini-meadows to enjoy for many years. Read this story about a fourth-grade class that created a mini-meadow next to their school playground.

1   After ten months of careful planning and hard work, the students in Mrs. Monroe's fourth grade class were thrilled. Their mini-meadow was now an active habitat at the edge of the school playground! Butterflies fluttered about, and Jose noticed that a small spider had built a web near the Prairie Sagebrush he had planted. While the children observed the wildlife on that warm May afternoon, they happily reflected on the steps they had taken to produce their busy garden space.

2   Mrs. Monroe, their science teacher, had informed the class about their mini-meadow project when school had started back in August. She explained that they would select and develop an area of land on the school grounds that would support a habitat made up of grasses, wildflowers, and other plants. At first, the students were worried that they would not have the time to create a successful meadow, but when Mrs. Monroe explained that they would use native plants that need little extra care, they were eager to start working.

3   First, the class decided on the best place in which to grow their meadow. Kelsie wanted the meadow to grow right next to the front entrance of the building so visitors could enjoy the natural view before entering the school. *Unfortunately,* nearby shade trees kept that area from getting much sunlight, which was needed for their meadow to grow well. The class brainstormed some possible sites and finally decided that the area to the left of the playground was best. It had full sunlight, the soil drained easily, and small grasses and plants were already growing there.

4   After deciding that their meadow would need to be 15 feet square in size, the students discussed the amount of seed they needed to purchase and what kinds of plants they should buy for the space. Mrs. Monroe reminded everyone that native plants, or plants found naturally in the area, grow best. Michael and James looked up information about native plants on the Internet and shared their findings. There were so many varieties to choose from! As well as growing shrubs and grasses, the students wanted to grow beautiful wildflowers to add color to the meadow. The wildflowers would attract bees and other wildlife, too.

5   By late September, the class had purchased enough plants and seeds for their meadow. Some helpful parents volunteered time, including Maria's father, who mowed the area as short as possible. The students then raked away the grass clippings in order to *expose* more soil. They planted some small shrubs, and they had fun mixing wildflower seeds with potting soil and then throwing the seeds out onto the prepared area. For the first few weeks after planting, they kept the meadow moist to make sure the plants established themselves in their new space.

6   Mrs. Monroe took her class out to the meadow frequently throughout the year to observe and take notes. By November, the meadow was showing many signs of growth. The students knew they would have to wait until early spring for their wildflowers to bloom, but it was well worth the wait. The mini-meadow filled with color by the middle of March, and bees merrily buzzed about, helping to pollinate the flowers.

7   In May, as the school year came to a close, the students looked back on their mini-meadow project. It had taken time and effort to create the meadow, but now they could see that the space would provide years of enjoyment for everyone at the school. Mrs. Monroe noted that in a few years' time, it would be a full-grown meadow. Abigail piped up that she would be sure to return to visit the meadow at that time. Many of the other students said they would visit then, too. They were all proud of their creation!

A

Mini-Meadow Questions

Use "Mini-Meadow" passage to answer questions 1-10.

1. Paragraph 5 tells mostly about

    A. how students raked away grass clippings

    B. why it was important to keep the soil moist

    C. how students and parents prepared and planted the area

    D. how students mixed wildflower seeds with potting soil

2. Which words in paragraph 5 help the reader to know what expose means?

    A. throwing the seeds

    B. raked away

    C. purchased enough

    D. small shrubs

3. How were the students able to choose which plants to grow in the mini-meadow?

    A. Some students looked up information on the Internet

    B. They asked their parents to choose the plants

    C. The students decided to choose only wildflowers

    D. They picked plants that would grow best in shade

4. Which sentence from the story shows the students enjoyed the mini-meadow?

    A. There were so many varieties to choose from!

    B. First, the class decided on the best place in which to grow their meadow.

    C. It had full sunlight, the soil drained easily, and small grasses and plants were already growing there.

    D. They were all proud of their creation!

5. Based on the information in this story, the reader can tell the students in Mrs. Monroe's class

    A. work well together

    B. think their school needs a better playground

    C. have always been proud of their school

    D. are ready for fifth grade

6. What is the purpose of this story?

    A. To explain how students can work together to create a mini-meadow

    B. To describe the students in Mrs. Monroe's class

    C. To tell how a mini-meadow helps wildlife

    D. To inform why it is important to grow wildflowers

7. In paragraph 3, the word unfortunately means

  A. with help
  B. not paid
  C. not with good luck
  D. with good luck

8. Who mowed the area as short as possible when preparing the mini-meadow?

  A. Maria
  B. Mrs. Monroe
  C. Michael and James
  D. Maria's father

9. From what the reader learns about mini-meadows, which statement does not make sense?

  A. It is best to locate a mini-meadow in an area with full sunlight
  B. Bees are attracted to plants in a mini-meadow
  C. Wildflowers start to emerge soon after planting the seeds
  D. Creating a mini-meadow takes planning time

10. Why did students rake away the grass clippings before planting shrubs and seeds?

  A. They wanted to expose more soil
  B. It helped keep the area moist
  C. It added fifteen feet to the size of the mini-meadow
  D. It was fun to mix the clippings with the soil

A

What to Eat & When to Eat it Gameboard

Piece 1

On the following pages are the 4 sections of the gameboard.
Just remove the pages and tape them together as shown below.

**Piece 1, on the back of this page, represents
the bottom right corner of the game board.**

A

Daytime

Nighttime

Nighttime

Berries

Finish!!

Trim Here

What to Eat & When to Eat it Gameboard

Piece 2

Piece 2, on the back of this page, represents the top right corner of the game board.

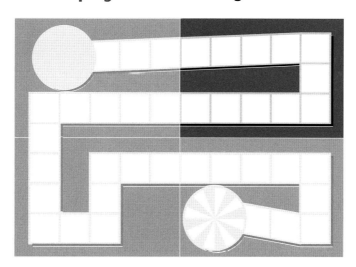

A

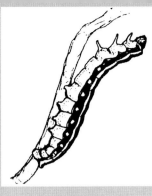

Trim Here

Daytime

Daytime

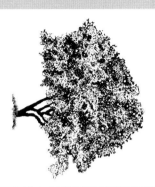

Berries

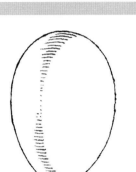

Nighttime

Daytime

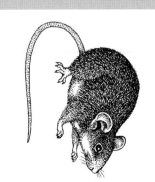

What to Eat & When to Eat it Gameboard

Piece 3

Piece 3, on the back of this page, represents the bottom left corner of the game board.

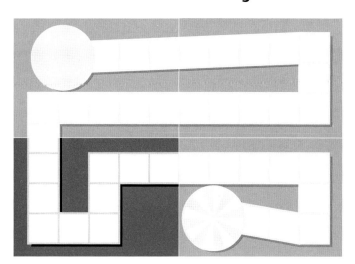

A

Trim Here

Nighttime

Nighttime

Daytime

Seeds

What to Eat & When to Eat it Gameboard

Piece 4

Piece 4, on the back of this page, represents the top left corner of the game board.

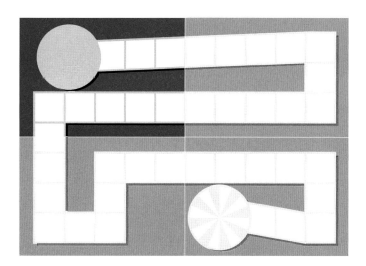

A

What to Eat & When to Eat it

Start

Berries

Nighttime

Habitat Basics

A

Habitat Basics

All wildlife needs an appropriate combination of food, water, cover, and places to raise young. Therefore Schoolyard Habitats sites must include these four essential habitat elements specific to the local wildlife they seek to support and attract. Some areas of the schoolyard might already be visited by wildlife; these areas may naturally provide some or all essential habitat elements. If so, consider enhancing or restoring habitat that already exists. *It is just as important to restore and conserve existing habitat areas as it is to create new habitat on the schoolyard.*

Providing a wide variety of appropriate habitat elements will attract a diversity of wildlife to your schoolyard. Following are a few brief suggestions on how to provide food, water, cover and places for wildlife to raise young on your schoolgrounds. Accompanying each habitat component is a preview of the corresponding portion of the Schoolyard Habitats Application which your school will eventually be completing. (To learn more about certification and to view the application in its entirety, see page 219).

Food

The ideal Schoolyard Habitats plan uses vegetation to supply as much food as possible to meet the year-round needs of many local species. Shrubs, trees, and other plants produce foods, such as acorns, nuts, berries, and other seeds. Leaves, buds, catkins, nectar, and pollen are also important food sources.

Locally native plants are the basis for the natural food chain in any given ecosystem. Therefore, it is important that any Schoolyard Habitats plantings consist of locally native plant species that include trees, shrubs, perennials, and annuals. Contact a Cooperative Extension office, local garden center, state non-game wildlife program, nature center, or the National Wildlife Federation field office closest to you for recommendations about the best locally native wildlife plants (See Native Plants, page XI).

While plants are maturing, and in areas with cold winters, natural food sources can be supplemented with food for birds. The best foods for feeders are sunflower, safflower, proso millet seed, niger seed, and suet. In warm months, sugar water in regularly cleaned humming bird feeders supplements the nectar and insects that flowers provide. Feeder maintenance is an excellent ongoing student project.

Water

Throughout the year, wildlife needs water for drinking, bathing, and in some cases, breeding. Water can be supplied in a birdbath or other shallow dish, a small pond, a shallow wetland, or stream. While vegetation holds droplets from rain or morning dew, a more constant, reliable source of water is needed by many wildlife species and therefore is recommended in Schoolyard Habitats sites.

Butterflies, birds, frogs, and toads often prefer to use shallow, puddle-like water sources. Create puddles by filling a shallow basin with clean sand; sink the basin into the ground in a sunny spot within your garden. Keep it flooded so that some of the water and sand spill over the edge at different times of the season.

An elevated birdbath may protect birds from cats and other predators, and can be an attractive addition to your Schoolyard Habitats site. Place birdbaths near an overhanging branch or a nearby bush to provide a quick escape route for songbirds from predators but not so close that predators have a good hiding place within pouncing range. The bath should be no deeper than 3" and have gently sloping sides, with water less than 2" deep. In summer heat, be sure to replace water regularly and to keep birdbaths

Schoolyard Habitats Application

A. FOOD: Plantings and Feeders

Food is best provided for wildlife naturally (nuts, nectar, berries, pollen, and buds). The best source of naturally occurring food is found in plants native to your region. Care should also be taken to provide year-round food sources for local wildlife. Briefly list the food available for wildlife at your site, if it is provided naturally or as a supplement, and if it is provided through native plants. Discovering which plants are native is an important part of the learning process in Schoolyard Habitats work. If you are unsure whether the plants on your schoolyard are native, involve your students and Habitat Team in research to find out!

Food Type	Provided By	Visited By	This Plant is Native
Ex. berries	dogwood	Robins	•

A

Basic Steps for Building a Pond

Basic Steps for Building a Pond:

1. **Check Local Regulations.** Many schools are concerned with the liability issues of having open water on their campuses. Before planning pond construction, check school district and municipality guidelines. These are usually easy-to-follow regulations regarding the size, depth, and location of schoolyard water features.

2. **Observe the natural flow of water on the property.** The best time to do this is right after it rains. The ideal site for the pond may be where water naturally accumulates on the schoolyard. Make sure that the site does not receive excess nutrients from compost piles, fertilizers placed on lawns, or street runoff.

3. **Choose Pond Structure.** One of several options available for creating pond structures is to use a commercially available flexible liner. Create a basin by excavating the soil and providing a gradually sloping beach area so that amphibians and other wildlife species can leave and enter the pond easily. Many schools choose to provide an overflow "wetland" area next to the pond (a place for water to flow during excessive precipitation), to support additional types of plants and wildlife, and to thereby provide greater educational opportunities.

4. **Install.** Before laying the liner, pad the hole with a layer of sand or some old carpeting, and then put the liner in place. Secure with rocks. Before filling pond with water, check to see if the local municipality uses chlorine or chloramine. Chlorine will dissipate after one week, but a neutralizer is necessary in order to adjust chloramine levels.

5. **Add Water and Vegetation.** Cover the surface of your pond with a layer of leaves. These will sink to the bottom and form an organic layer and provide habitat for microorganisms. Place plenty of plants, rocks and tree branches in the pond as emergent structures so wildlife have places to sun and to seek cover. A good way to mimic nature's recipe for a healthy pond is to add a bucket of water from a nearby natural pond. Do not stock the pond with fish. Wildlife will eventually find the pond on their own. If aquatic plants are added, be sure to add only native species—these will offer the maximum benefits to local wildlife. Avoid exotic ornamentals.

6. **Take Safety Precautions.** Address safety concerns by educating students about potential risks. Student-made educational signs posted close to the pond are a great way to call attention to the presence of water. Another way to slow foot traffic and create a boundary between the pond and a playground area, for instance, is to install low fences or benches around the pond. Small ponds may also be created in courtyards where students are always visible. Another solution is to create a deep basin, and back-fill much of the basin with large rocks. This type of pond will support small aquatic species while remaining quite shallow (which will allay fears of potential danger to students).

clean. In winter, if temperatures drop well below freezing, use a birdbath heater or remove ice in the morning and refill with water daily.

If a creek, stream, pond or wetland already exists on the schoolyard, consider enhancing or restoring that area. If a water body is not present, many schools choose to create a pond as part of their Schoolyard Habitats project. Ponds not only help support a greater diversity of wildlife, but expand opportunities for hands-on teaching and learning. Students with schoolyard ponds learn directly about everything from aquatic insects to water quality to physical science. A small pond built into the ground can provide water for drinking and bathing as well as cover and reproductive areas for small fish, amphibians, insects, and reptiles. Many birds and amphibians rely on insects that spend part or all of their

life in the water. Observing naturally occurring local ponds will help students learn about the characteristics and life

Schoolyard Habitats Application PREVIEW

B. WATER: Drinking, Bathing

Wildlife needs water daily and throughout the year. An elevated birdbath may protect birds from cats and other predators, while a shallow, wide-rimmed dish will provide water for small animals when placed on the ground near shrubbery or other cover. A small pond set into the ground can provide not only water for drinking and bathing, but cover and reproductive areas for small fish, frogs, insects, and reptiles.

We provide water: ☐ Throughout the Year ☐ Seasonally

We provide water in: ☐ Bird Bath ☐ Pond
☐ Stream ☐ Spring Water Garden
☐ Water Garden ☐ Water Dripping into a Bird Bath

A

 Appendix

requirements of locally native aquatic plants and animals.

Some people are hesitant about creating a pond because they associate ponds with mosquitoes. Though some may see them as a nuisance, mosquitoes do help support many natural predators such as bats and dragonflies. In healthy ecosystems with plenty of native vegetation, mosquitoes usually do not pose any problems. If mosquito larvae are a concern, eliminate standing water by installing a small circulating pump.

Many certified National Wildlife Federation Schoolyard Habitats sites have installed ponds on their schoolgrounds. Whether they have removed a concrete

courtyard, or simply converted an unused corner of grassy lawn, they are all now enjoying the wildlife that visit and make their homes in these ponds, and the instructional possibilities the pond provides.

Cover

Wildlife needs protective cover from heat, cold, wind, rain, and predators. Many plants that offer food can also provide valuable escape cover for wildlife. Densely branched shrubs, evergreens, grasses, as well as hollow trees—upright and fallen—rock piles, brush piles, and stone walls can all provide cover for many animal species.

Schoolyard Habitats Application PREVIEW

C. COVER: Places to Hide

The ideal wildlife habitat area will include plants ranging in size and density from evergreen ground cover to tall, mature trees. This variety of plant life will assist a range of animals in selecting the appropriate cover they need for feeding, hiding, courting, and nesting. Hollow logs, brush piles, and stone walls can add to the range of cover you provide.

Deciduous Shrubs/Trees	Qty	Evergreen Shrubs/Trees	Qty

We provide cover for wildlife in the following manner:

☐ Brush Piles   ☐ Log Piles   ☐ Rock Piles/Walls

☐ Ground Covers   ☐ Meadow, Scrub, or Prairie Patch

☐ Other (describe): _____

The ideal wildlife habitat area includes plants ranging in size and density from low ground cover to tall, mature trees. Arranging plants in groups that mimic the growth of plant communities (rather than in isolated islands) will increase the amount of cover provided. Increasing the diversity of plant species will increase the diversity of wildlife that is supported; this variety of plant life provides birds and other animals with a wide array of appropriate cover for feeding, hiding, courting, and nesting activities.

To add to the types of cover on the schoolyard, students can construct and erect nesting boxes for the resident or migratory songbirds, ducks, and bats that live in the area (these structures are also available commercially). Each type of wildlife nesting box has specific requirements; it is important to identify the overall box size, entrance size, design, and placement needed in order to successfully attract specific species. Following these specifications will both ensure that the box is usable by the intended species, and that the box is not unduly vulnerable to that species' predators.

Resources for Nest Box Plans and Information:

■ The U.S. Fish and Wildlife Service maintains an excellent list of how to attract and support 13 bird species through nest boxes: *http://migratorybirds.fws.gov/pamphlet/pamplets.html*

■ Bat Conservation International provides detailed plans on its website for constructing bat boxes, bat conservation issues. Videos, books, and many other resources can also be ordered online: www.batcons.org

■ The North American Bluebird Society provides thorough information about bluebirds and supporting local populations through bluebird boxes: *www.nabluebirdsociety.org*

Places to Raise Young

To be complete, habitat areas must include safe places in which wildlife can raise their young. Examples include appropriate areas for nesting, specific plants upon which butterfly larvae depend, and the security of pond water for tadpoles.

Consider providing places to raise young through both vegetation and human-made devices. Attach birdhouses and nesting shelves to posts, trees, or buildings. Maintain as many snags (dead, standing trees with hollow cavities) as

A

possible. Plant dense pockets of shrubbery to provide safe areas for many species of wildlife.

Some of our most interesting animals require a body of water as a safe haven for their young. Many salamanders, frogs, toads, and insects, like dragonflies and water boatmen, begin life in water and are unlikely to prosper on the schoolyard without the safe, healthy water environments that a clean stream or small pond can offer.

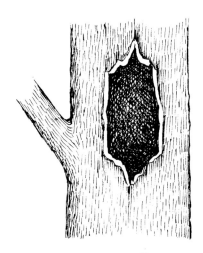

Schoolyard Habitats Application

D. PLACES TO RAISE YOUNG

A more specific kind of cover is needed to make your wildlife habitat complete. These are areas for courtship and for nurturing young animals and include safe areas for nests, specific plants upon which butterfly caterpillars depend, and the shallow water security that tadpoles find in a pond.

We provide the following for nesting birds, denning mammals, egg-laying reptiles and amphibians, fish, butterflies, and other insects and invertebrates:

Large Trees	Small Trees	Shrub Masses

☐ Trees with Nest/Den Cavities   ☐ Dens in Ground/Rock

☐ Water Garden/Pond   ☐ Nesting Boxes

☐ Nesting Shelves   ☐ Meadow, Prairie, or Scrub Patch

☐ Other (describe):

A

Schoolyard Habitats Certification

We strongly encourage schools to certify their Schoolyard Habitats projects with the National Wildlife Federation. We want to hear about your project and give you the recognition you and your school community deserve. We look forward to receiving your application for certification as an official Schoolyard Habitats sites, and to welcoming your school into our dynamic network of certified schools.

Frequently asked questions about the certification process

■ How do I know when I'm ready to certify my habitat project?

You are ready to certify after a team has been involved in planning and providing at least a few types of food, water, cover, and places to raise young on your schoolgrounds, and when the site is being used as a teaching tool.

■ What are the benefits of certifying?

Certifying your site will bring media attention and national recognition for your school community's hard work. Also, once you are certified, you can enjoy the Schoolyard Habitats listserv and quarterly newsletter, and be eligible to order a Schoolyard Habitats sign for your outdoor classroom. Certification brings

your school into a dynamic network of certified schools, and gives you access to special resources and information from the National Wildlife Federation.

■ How many other people have certified their schoolgrounds?

Over 1500 schools (as of September 2001), representing thousands of students, parents, teachers, administrators, and community members, are currently certified as official Schoolyard Habitats sites, representing 49 states and a few sites abroad.

■ How do I apply?

Simply fill out the application and mail it in to our office. Be sure to include photos, if available. (Applications can also be downloaded from our website at www.nwf.org/schoolyardhabitats). Within 4-8 weeks, you will hear from us regarding your certification. We look forward to learning about your project, and to welcoming you into the Schoolyard Habitats network.

■ Can I include photographs?

Yes! Please do. Photos help us learn more about your project; we can also inspire and educate others by posting photos of Schoolyard Habitats projects around the country on our website. We especially enjoy "before" and "after" photos, to get a better sense of your progress. A photo release form must accompany photos which include people's faces. The form follows the SYH application in this manual (page 226); feel free to copy as necessary, and submit these forms with your completed application and photographs.

A

 **Appendix**

schoolyard habitats **Application** *for* **Certification**
NATIONAL WILDLIFE FEDERATION®

School/Learning Center Name _____

Principal/Director _____

Contact Name (if different) _____

Address _____

City _____

State/Province _____ County _____ Zip/Postal Code _____

School Telephone _____ Contact Telephone (if different) _____

Fax _____ Contact E-mail Address _____

Office Use:
Habitat # _____
Date Received _____
Certified _____
C.S. _____
Key Words _____
Source Code _____

Would you like to be added to the Schoolyard Habitats listserv? ☐ Yes ☐ No

School Website Address _____ *Does your website feature your SYH project?* ☐ Yes ☐ No

Would you like your Schoolyard Habitats site featured on the NWF website? ☐ Yes ☐ No

Grade Level(s) Served by School/Learning Center: _____

Ages of Students Actively Involved in SYH Project: _____

Size (Sq. Ft. or Acres) of SYH Project Site: _____

How did you hear about the Schoolyard Habitats program? _____

A Schoolyard Habitats project can be an incredible addition to your school campus and local community for many years to come. After reading the Schoolyard Habitats Planning Guide, please complete all five sections of this application, showing the steps you have taken to create the habitat area and how it is used as a learning site. Incomplete applications may not be accepted. For assistance with the application, contact the SYH Program Staff at wildlife@nwf.org or call 1-800-822-9919.

I)   Project Description/Goals

Please briefly describe current projects and future goals for the Schoolyard Habitats site. Include the process that occurred during the development of your habitat and the educational objectives of this project.

_____

_____

_____

_____

II) Habitat Team Structure

The team should represent a variety of people (i.e. not all team members should be teachers). List the key participants involved with the habitat project and the segment of the school community they represent.

Team Member Name: Representing:

_____   _____

_____   _____

_____   _____

_____   _____

_____   _____

III) Habitat Components

Locally native plants provide the widest range of seasonal habitat benefits to wildlife. If we want not only to attract wildlife, but to help restore the diversity of our local ecosystems, we must bring back our locally native plants. The National Wildlife Federation strongly encourages the use of native plants.

A. FOOD: *Plantings and Feeders*

Food is best provided for wildlife naturally (nuts, nectar, berries, pollen, and buds). The best source of naturally occurring food is found in plants native to your region. Care should also be taken to provide year-round food sources for local wildlife. Briefly list the food available for wildlife at your site, if it is provided naturally or as a supplement, and if it is provided through native plants. Discovering which plants are native is an important part of the learning process in Schoolyard Habitats work. If you are unsure whether the plants on your schoolyard are native, involve your students and Habitat Team in research to find out!

			This plant is native:	
Food Type:	Provided By:	Visited By:	Yes	No
ex: berries	*Cotoneaster*	*Hermit Thrushes, Robins, & Bluebirds*	☒	☐
_____	_____	_____	☐	☐
_____	_____	_____	☐	☐
_____	_____	_____	☐	☐
_____	_____	_____	☐	☐
_____	_____	_____	☐	☐

B. WATER: *Drinking, Bathing*

Wildlife needs water daily and throughout the year. An elevated birdbath may protect birds from cats and other predators, while a shallow, wide-rimmed dish will provide water for small animals when placed on the ground near shrubbery or other cover. A small pond set into the ground can provide not only water for drinking and bathing, but cover and reproductive areas for small fish, frogs, insects and reptiles.

We provide water: ☐ Throughout the Year   ☐ Seasonally

We provide water in: ☐ Bird Bath   ☐ Pond

                      ☐ Spring   ☐ Water Garden

                      ☐ Water Dripping into a Bird Bath   ☐ Stream

                      ☐ Other (describe): _____

A

C. COVER: *Places to Hide*

The ideal wildlife habitat area will include plants ranging in size and density from evergreen ground cover to tall, mature trees. This variety of plant life will assist a range of animals in selecting the appropriate cover they need for feeding, hiding, courting and nesting. Hollow logs, brush piles, and stone walls can add to the range of cover you provide.

We provide cover for wildlife in the following manner:

Deciduous Shrubs/Trees:	Number	Evergreen Shrubs/Trees:	Number:
_____	_____	_____	_____
_____	_____	_____	_____
_____	_____	_____	_____

☐ Brush Piles ☐ Log Piles ☐ Rock Piles/Walls ☐ Ground Covers

☐ Meadow, Scrub, or Prairie Patch ☐ Other (describe): _____

D. PLACES TO RAISE YOUNG

A more specific kind of cover is needed to make your wildlife habitat complete. These are areas for courtship and for nurturing young animals and include safe areas for nests, specific plants upon which butterfly caterpillars depend, and the shallow water security that tadpoles find in a pond.

We provide the following for nesting birds, denning mammals, egg-laying reptiles and amphibians, fish, butterflies, and other insects and invertebrates:

Large Trees:	Small Trees:	Shrub Masses:
_____	_____	_____
_____	_____	_____
_____	_____	_____

☐ Trees with Nest/Den Cavities ☐ Dens in Ground/Rock

☐ Water Garden/Pond ☐ Nesting Boxes

☐ Nesting Shelves ☐ Meadow, Prairie, or Scrub Patch

☐ Other (describe): _____

IV) Site Diagram and Project Documentation

Please enclose a sketch or landscape design on 8.5" x 11" paper to visually explain the components of your Schoolyard Habitats site. Please make note of which elements are currently in place, and which will be added in the future. Indicate any features created to make the habitat accessible to students with disabilities (i.e. pathways, raised planting beds, etc.). We are unable to return all materials; please keep a duplicate copy for your records.

We encourage you to send before and after photos of your Schoolyard Habitats site, as well as photos which demonstrate student and community involvement with the project. Please label all photos with your school name, city, state, and approximate dates when the photos were taken. All photos must be accompanied by a release form. Please download a copy of the release form from our website (or contact our office to request a copy if you plan to include photos with your application). We are unable to return materials sent to us, so please be sure to keep duplicates for your records.

V) Widening the Classroom Walls: *Curriculum Use*

Please submit additional pages as needed.

A. Describe how you are using your Schoolyard Habitats site for cross-curriculum learning. How do you meet state/local benchmarks and standards of learning through use of your habitat site?

B. How many teachers at your school are currently using the Schoolyard Habitats site as an educational tool?

C. What steps have you taken or do you plan to take in order to increase the usage (by students and teachers) of your Schoolyard Habitats site?

D. Have educators at your school written up lessons or curriculum for use in the Schoolyard Habitats site or to accompany the project? Please describe.

E. What resources have been helpful in the planning and instructional use of your Schoolyard Habitats project (e.g., Project Wild, Project Learning Tree, NAAEE's VINE program)?

F. What other types of resources would be useful to the future development and use of your Schoolyard Habitats site?

VI) Maintenance

Briefly describe your maintenance plan, both during the school year, as well as during the summer months.

Thank you for your interest and participation in the Schoolyard Habitats Program. Please:

- Allow 6-8 weeks for processing of the application.
- Be sure to save copies of all materials you submit as they will not be returned.
- **Please submit this application with the $15 Program Enrollment Fee to cover our processing and handling costs.**
- If submitting photos, please enclose a photo release form (see IV. Site Diagram and Project Documentation).
- All submissions must be sent together in one 9" x 12" envelope.

Please send your submission to: **Schoolyard Habitats Program**
National Wildlife Federation
11100 Wildlife Center Dr.
Reston, VA 20190-5362

NATIONAL
WILDLIFE
FEDERATION®
www.nwf.org™

A

 **Appendix**

NATIONAL WILDLIFE FEDERATION

APPLICATION FOR CERTIFICATION

PHOTO RELEASE | **Schoolyard Habitats® Program**

I understand that photographs are sometimes taken of Schoolyard Habitats® Program participants by participants, participants' family members, and NWF staff. I hereby grant permission to National Wildlife Federation, to use, copyright, publish, and republish, in any form:

1. Any photograph(s) taken of myself or any minor of whom I am the parent or guardian, participating in the Schoolyard Habitats Program held on_____[day, month and year of the program]; or

2. Any photograph(s) taken by myself that I voluntarily submit to the National Wildlife Federation. The submission of any photograph in support of a Schoolyard Habitats Program is not required for processing an application and I have voluntarily chosen to submit this (these) photograph(s).

I understand that such photographs may be used or published by NWF for purposes of advertising and promoting NWF's Schoolyard Habitats program or for any other purpose that NWF deems appropriate, in any and all media including, but not limited to, printed and electronic media. Neither my name, nor the name of the minor(s), if applicable, shall be published in connection with NWF's use of any photograph(s). I further understand that no payment will be made for NWF's use of such photographs and that it is not possible for NWF to return any original photographs that I may send to NWF on my own initiative.

I/we will be participating in the National Wildlife Federation's Schoolyard Habitats Program at: _____. I/we have read the above terms carefully and acknowledge my/our informed consent to its terms.

Participant _____ Date _____
(and Parent or Guardian, if participant is under 18)

Please complete the following information (please print clearly):

Adult Participant's Full Name_____

Minor(s) Participating in the NWF Schoolyard Habitats Program under my supervision (if applicable):

Minor's Full Name _____

Minor's Full Name _____

Minor's Full Name _____

Minor's Full Name _____

Acknowledgments

227

Acknowledgements

Wildlife Gardener Project Coordinator and Editor

Randy L. Seagraves, Curriculum Director, National Junior Master Gardener Program

Authors

 Michelle Meche, Extension Assistant, Texas Cooperative Extension,
The Texas A&M University System

Randy L. Seagraves

Lisa Whittlesey, Program Coordinator, National Junior Master Gardener Program

Cindy Klemmer, Ph.D, Manager, Center for Teaching and Learning,
Chicago Botanic Garden

Contributors

Bethe Gilbert Almeras, Sr. Coordinator - Schoolyard Habitats Program,
National Wildlife Federation

Sharon Katz Cooper, Curriculum Specialist, National Wildlife Federation

Susan O'Neil, Teacher, College Station Independent School District

Reviewers

Craig Tufts, Chief Naturalist, National Wildlife Federation

Stephanie Stowell, Senior Manager for Educator Programs,
National Wildlife Federation

Bethe Gilbert Almeras

Sharon Katz Cooper

Douglas F. Welsh, Ph.D., Professor and Extension Horticulturist,
Texas Cooperative Extension, The Texas A&M University System

Bastiaan "Bart" M. Drees, Professor, Extension Entomologist
and Regents Fellow, Department of Entomology, Texas A&M University

Kirk O. Winemiller, Professor, Department of Wildlife and
Fisheries Sciences, Texas A&M University

Lead Artwork
Jackson "T-Bone" Price, Art Director, Texas Transportation Institute,
The Texas A&M University System

Artwork
Patricia Wynne
TAMU Agricultural Communications

Layout and Design
Thomas Gordon, Pilot Light Studios

Copy Editor
Lisa Price, JP Creative

Photographs
University Photographic Services
Randy L. Seagraves
National Wildlife Federation

Photography Models
Crystal Knotts	**Alex Becker**	**Haley Fortenberry**
Kyle Ray	**James Hernandez**	**Hyunjin Koh**
Katelyn Clark	**Zabrina Sanchez**	**Kami Harris**
Tayler Millhollon	**Reece Nicholson**	**Bennie Clayton**
Ryan Williams	**Lauren Carstens**	**Cody Erickson**

Pilot Leaders and Sites
Sheri Hartshorn – Cascade, ID　　**Sheryl Nolen** – Conroe, TX
Gerry Hernandez – Colusa, CA　　**Beth Reidman** – Brookville, IN
Debbie Czarnopys – White - Dubois, IL　**Kelli Basset** – Hillsboro, IL
Tersea Glover – Mt. Vernon, IL　　**Shelia Thomas** – Ottawa, IL
Beck Hoerr – Pekin, IL　　**Kristi H. Schlegel** – Aiken, SC
Dr. Dean L. Crews – Warrenville, SC　**Juli Hughes** – Ackerman, MS
Becky Settlage – Weiser, ID　　**Diana Mendelsohn** – South Bend, IN
Nancey Cress – Marion, VA　　**Mamie Taylor, Dana Smith** – Onancoc, VA
Connie Hicks – Dillwyn, VA　　**Dianna Tibbs, Anne Richardson,**
Mary E. Gardner – Tupelo, MS　　**Leslie Davidson** – Marion, VA

Participating Extension Agencies

University of Illinois Extension Service
Monica David, Illinois Junior Master Gardener Coordinator

University of Idaho Extension Service
Kevin Laughlin, Idaho Junior Master Gardener Coordinator

Mississippi State University Extension Service
Lelia Scott Kelley, Mississippi Junior Master Gardener Coordinator

Purdue Extension
Kathryn Orvis, Indiana Junior Master Gardener Coordinator

Texas Cooperative Extension
Dee McKenna, Texas Junior Master Gardener Coordinator

Virgina Cooperative Extension
Joe Hunnings, Virgina Junior Master Gardener Coordinator

Clemson Extension
William Hair , South Carolina Junior Master Gardener Coordinator

University of California Agriculture and Natural Resources
Susan Gloeckler, Cailifornia Junior Master Gardener State Coordinator

Special Thanks to:

The kids and leaders across the country contributing to the
piloting of this curriculum
Sonnie Feagley for her organizational talents and office support
David Cain and his third grade class for serving as models for this curriculum
The expertise and zeal offered by the staff of the **Schoolyard Habitats Program and
the rest of the team at the National Wildlife Federation.**

*The Wildlife Gardener curriculum is made possible in part through the
generous contribution of **Dora Roberts Foundation.***